GETTING TO
DID!

How To Get Rid Of Your big but
And Live A life Without Regrets

EDWIN CROZIER

10 digit ISBN 0-9777829-2-1
13 digit ISBN 978-0-9777-8292-5

Printed in the United States of America

Thank you to my *YES MEN and WOMEN*

Special thanks to Marita, my wife. You hold me accountable when no one else will. You help my dreams become realities and help me
GET TO DID.

Also, to the amazing members of Let's Talk Franklin of Franklin, TN, whose openness, honesty and listening ears have helped me develop myself and this message.

To Steve and Carla Duffy whose inspiration and motivation kept me moving to *DID!* with this book.

To Clay Gentry whose encouragement pushed me to get this book off my computer and on to the bookshelf.

Finally, I want to thank you, dear reader, for listening to my message and helping me spread it to others.

A Word from the Author

Sam's world was crumbling. Perhaps you have been there. Perhaps you are there. Perhaps you want to avoid getting there. Is your life a meandering stream of regrets and missed opportunities? Or do you just want to make sure it never becomes one? Whatever the case, this book is for you.

Sam learns from Dave and his friends how to *DID IT*, reaching his potential by avoiding *"COULDA, SHOULDA, WOULDA"* and getting rid of his big *BUT.* This is Sam's story.

However, it will help you with your story as well. In whatever way you relate to this story, I invite you to make this book a workbook. Write in it. Highlight it. Underline it. Throughout this story, Sam is given several homework assignments by his new advisors. I encourage you to use those forms as well.

Read the entire story to get the big picture of *DID!* Then read it again, going through the story just as Sam *DID*, filling out the forms and exercises as they fit in your story.

My sincere hope is Sam's story will be a gift to you and a help to your life.

Thank you,

Edwin L. Crozier

Sam's Story

Sam's Crumbling World

Sam's world was crumbling. Have you been there? Are you there? Are you afraid you are going there? Then you know how Sam felt. Not that his world had ever really been that big or that stable. But it had been his. It had been comfortable. *Had been*. Now it was collapsing.

Sam was 49. He had been semi-happily married to Susan for 25 of those years. His oldest son, Sam Jr. was 23 and a recent graduate from Sam's alma mater. Sarah, the lone female, was 20. Scott was 17 and would be starting his senior year in high school in just a few months. The youngest, Sid, was 14 and going into the eighth grade.

Seven months ago, Sam was at the top of his world. A few years earlier, he had been promoted to Vice President of Sales in the company that had pursued him as a salesman when he was 32. He and Susan had finally bought that bigger home. Since Sam had been given a company car, he bought Susan the Lexus she always wanted. Things were good. But then Sam's company was sold. The buyer wanted to keep several workers in Sam's company, but wanted to rely on her own management team. Sam no longer fit. She let Sam go the week after Christmas.

He was given a decent severance package, promised a good recommendation and then politely escorted with his box of office paraphernalia off company property, where he called Susan to pick him up because he was no longer allowed to use the company car. She handled the news relatively well. Sam cried for a week.

For months he called it his worst Christmas present ever. However, in years to come he called it his best.

Realizing Susan's income, supplemented by the severance package and their meager savings, could support their lifestyle for about a year, he started looking for another job. "Really," he thought, "I don't know why I've been so depressed. I'm highly qualified. I have a Bachelors degree in business and marketing and a Masters in accounting. I've worked for the same company for 17 years. My track record is good. Who wouldn't want to hire me?"

Sam, however, learned that "overqualified" was the politically correct and lawsuit safe euphemism for "too old." None of the companies to which he applied wanted 49-year-olds with good track records. They were too busy head hunting 32-year-olds with promising futures.

Though he was only halfway through his severance package, Sam felt he was at the end of his rope. As he often did when particularly stressed and depressed, he manicured his lawn. Keeping his yard "green and pristine," as he called it, was about the only joy he had. It gave him time alone to think, provided a sense of accomplishment and, if nothing else, hid from the neighbors the turmoil going on inside the house.

He had just finished and was sitting down on his back deck with a glass of ice water, when his neighbor, Dave, came around the corner of the house and said, "Hey Sam. How's the job hunt going?"

"Great Dave, just great. You trying to pour salt in the wounds?"

"Still no luck, huh? Keep trying. Something is bound to come up."

"I hope so, but I'm beginning to doubt it. Right now, however, I'm more ticked at Scott," Sam unloaded.

"What? I thought Scott was the good kid."

"He is, but we've been fighting a lot lately. He's going to be a senior this year and I've been on him to get his application in to the ol' alma mater. But he keeps putting it off. I told him if he keeps waiting, it'll be too late and he'll be stuck going to the local community college. Do you know what he said?" Without giving Dave time to answer, Sam continued, "He said, 'So? I'm not sure I want to go to your alma mater anyway.'" Sam gave an exasperated "you know how dumb kids can be sometimes look" to Dave, but Dave didn't respond.

Sam simply continued talking, "I told him I was only looking out for his own good. He needed to go to a good school, study hard, make good grades and then he could get a good secure job and provide for his family. You know what he said then?" Sam plunged on, "He said, 'You mean like you?' Talk about kicking a guy when he's down."

"Well, Sam, he does have a bit of a point. It's hard to take that kind of advice from a guy whose good secure job has left him so insecure."

Sam, his eyes wide, spluttered, "Well… yeah, I know. But I just want what's best for him. My dad went to that school and so did his dad. It's done all of us well. I mean, didn't you want Dave Jr. to go to your alma mater?"

"I guess I might have, if I had one. But, I never went to college. Don't get me wrong, I wanted Dave Jr. to go. I thought that was important, and I told him so. But I didn't think it was so important he should sacrifice what *he* thought was important."

Sam sat in stunned silence for a moment. Dave the most successful men he knew didn't even go to college? How could that happen? He owned several restaurants and a few apartment buildings. In fact, it had always amazed Sam that Dave lived in his neighborhood, when surely he could have afforded something much more. Dave and his wife Deborah always looked happy. In fact, despite their having been married over 40 years, Sam always had the impression they were newlyweds. He chalked that up to no longer having kids at home. On top of that, he had heard Dave's kids were also pretty successful.

"You never went to college?" Sam questioned, words tumbling out in gusts. "How on earth have you done so well? Did you get a big inheritance? I could sure use one." Sam slouched back in his chair.

Dave smiled slightly. "I guess you might say I got a big inheritance, but not the kind you're thinking of. I consider my dad one of the most successful men to have ever lived, but he never had much money. There were some things he always *DID* however. He always *DID* his best. He always *DID* what he enjoyed. And he always *DID* take care of us. He died while I was still in

> But he always *DID* his best.
>
> He always *DID* what he enjoyed.
>
> And he always *DID* take care of us.
>
> He *DID* leave me a legacy of knowing how to get things done.

high school." Dave paused, looked up and smiled again as though he had just relived some great moment. Then he continued, "He *DID* leave me a legacy of knowing how to get things done. That's why I'm successful. That's why I was able to start my first restaurant when I was 25 and then invest in several franchises over the years. That's why I was able to get into real estate investing. That's why I was able to quit working for money in my 40s."

"Yeah, I *coulda* started my own business, *but* I was newly married and I needed the benefits, you know what I mean?"

"Sure, I know," Dave responded. He continued after a brief pause, "Exactly what are those benefits doing for you now, Sam?"

"Well, I *shoulda* handled my money more wisely, *but* my wife and kids were always wanting more and I wanted to give them the best. You know, I wanted them to have what I never got."

"How much longer are you going to be able to do that, Sam?"

"Come on, Dave, I *woulda* got a job by now, *but* all those companies want young guys. I feel like I'm in my prime. Fifty is the new thirty, you know, *but* they think I should be put out to pasture. I wish I had done things differently, *but* hindsight is 20/20. I'll just have to live with my regrets. Right now I just need a job."

Dave fixed Sam with a hard gaze. He paused for a moment as if measuring the words in his mind before letting them slip out of his mouth. "Sam, if you want my advice, you need to get rid of your big *BUT*."

"What?!" Sam squawked nearly spilling his drink as he jumped forward in his chair. "You…you think my weight is holding me back?"

"Wrong 'butt,' pal. You're filled with *COULDAS*, *SHOULDAS* and *WOULDAS*. Then you cap them all off with a big *BUT*. That's why you've got so many regrets. You need to turn those into *CANS*, *SHALLS*, *WILLS* and *DID*. That was the inheritance my dad left me. He taught me to get rid of my big *BUT*, to reach my potential, getting past *COULDA, SHOULDA* and *WOULDA* and get things done. Or as I call it, *GET TO DID*. That's what's helped me be successful. That's what's helped me live a life without regrets."

"Wow…I think," Sam said, scratching his head. "I don't have any idea what you're talking about. Sounds like some kind of crazy PMA stuff we used to get from the home office."

Dave responded, "No, it's not just PMA and you probably do know what I'm talking about. You just don't realize it. You can't possibly have been as successful at sales as you have been without following some of the principles I like to share with people. You just don't realize how they apply to everything in life, even trying to make ends meet after losing your job. Somebody told me that Plato said all learning is really remembering. I don't really know what he meant by that. But I've found that when someone passes on a true principle to me, I really already knew it in my gut, I just needed someone to formulate it into words to give it power in my life.

"I've been watching you and hurting for you, Sam. I normally wait until someone asks me for advice to give it, but we've been friends for a while and I'd like to ask you to trust me and let me give you some real help. In the end, if you think it's crazy and my friends and I are just flukes or flakes, you can go back to hunting for a job your way."

Sam crossed his arms and cocked his head to one side. "So you think you *could* help me by *GETTING TO*...what was it you said?"

"*GETTING TO DID.* No, I *COULD* not. I steer clear of the *COULDAS.* Rather, I *CAN*, I *SHALL* and I *WILL.* In fact, consider it *DID.*"

Sam's face said it all; he didn't get it. "Dave, what you just said didn't make a lick of sense to me."

"Of course not. You don't know the tools yet. But if you'll let me give you just a few opportunities to talk with my *YES MEN* and me, you'll understand all of it."

"*YES MEN*? I already don't like the sound of this. I've never liked those kind of people."

19

"That's because you're thinking about a completely different kind of *YES MEN* than I am. But again, that'll be something you learn when you talk with my friends. How 'bout it?"

"Alright, Dave. This sounds crazy, but I think you must know what you're talking about. I mean, I guess it can't hurt," Sam gave a weak laugh, "When do we start? I only have about six months to get things on track or it's foreclosure and dog food time."

"Let's start in the morning. I'm already hav-ing coffee with one of my advisors then. I call him my *TRAINER*. I've stayed in touch with him for years because he helps me turn my *COULDA* into *CAN*. I'll let him know you're coming. I *CAN* get him to clear some time for you and let him teach you the first step on the journey to *DID*. Meet me in my driveway at 5:45."

The TRAINER

From COULDA to CAN

THE TRAINER

Sam told Susan he was getting up early to have coffee with Dave and a friend and that he thought Dave was going to help him find a job. He left it at that. He wasn't sure what all that *COULDA, SHOULDA, WOULDA* and *GETTING TO DID* stuff really meant and he did not want to sound like an idiot who had just latched on to some hare-brained scheme even if it did come from Dave. He especially did not want to tell her the whole point of this meeting was to help him get rid of his big *BUT*. Something told him she might not understand.

However, a few hours later, his excitement had worn off and Sam had trouble getting to sleep—but for different reasons than usual. He mentally argued with himself for several hours before finally sacking out.

This whole *GETTING TO DID* thing sounded odd. In fact, now that he thought about it, he should have just let Dave talk and then gone back to the classifieds to look for a job. All that *CAN, SHALL* and *WILL* stuff may be good for someone like Dave, *BUT* another call to his recruiter would be more helpful to Sam. Then he thought, "I can't argue with Dave's success. *BUT* it can't be as easy as Dave was suggesting."

*****

Since he didn't drift off to sleep until nearly one o'clock, the alarm came way too early for Sam. His habit of hitting the snooze button took over. Susan, however, nudged him and reminded him of his appointment. He thought briefly about calling Dave and saying he didn't feel good this morning and maybe they could do it later. However, if he wasn't all that excited about the meeting, he was at least pushed by his pride on keeping commitments and being punctual. Those were two keys he had taught sales reps for years.

He showered, shaved, dressed and headed out the door. As he walked up Dave's driveway at 5:44, the garage door slid open and Dave pulled out in what looked like a brand spanking new Mustang convertible with the top down. He stopped long enough to let Sam climb in.

"Midlife crisis?" Sam asked.

"Nope," Dave said with a mischievous grin. "Second childhood." Then he gunned it out of the driveway and they headed down the road.

"Ever been to *The Early Bird Cafe*, Sam?"

"No, what's that."

Dave chuckled. "You're in for a treat. It's this little breakfast and lunch spot. They roast their own coffee beans every day and they make these awesome sandwiches on Italian bread called paninis. My wife took me there once. I thought it was going to be one of those fru-fru restaurants for women. I was wrong. It's my favorite morning spot in town."

The conversation died down for a moment. Sam yawned and said, "I've been thinking, Dave. This can't be nearly as easy as you made it sound last night."

"Did I make it sound easy?" Dave replied. "Sorry 'bout that, Sam. You're right. Nothing you're going to learn from me or my friends is easy. Yes, it's easy to talk about. It's easy to write about. It's easy to hear and know it will work. In fact, like I said yesterday, most of what you are going to learn from us is stuff you probably learned in sales, you just didn't know you could apply it to real life. But it's not easy to do. Well, actually it is easy to do. The real problem is most of us just don't want to. Therefore it's extremely hard for most of us to *GET TO DID*. No, it's not easy. However, it works; if you will."

> "The real problem is most of us just don't want to. Therefore, it's extremely hard to *GET TO DID*. No, it's not easy. However, it works; if you will."

"I don't know, Dave, what if I can't do it? What if I'm not like you?"

"Sam, let me assure you, you're not like me and you don't have to be. However, you *CAN* do it."

"How do you know?"

"Because, *GETTING TO DID* is not about getting you to do something like everybody else or anybody else. It's not about getting you to be me. It's not about getting you to do something you can't do right now. It's about you learning to do what you *CAN*. Look," Dave pointed at a little café in a shopping strip, "we're here and there's my *TRAINER'S* truck. He'll explain more once we get inside."

Dave and Sam walked into the coffee shop. The smell of freshly roasted coffee mixed with eggs and sausage helped brighten Sam's outlook a little. "Hey, Dave," the two ladies working the counter said almost simultaneously.

"Hey, Tammy. Hey, Melinda. Two coffees this morning," Dave said wagging his finger from Sam to himself a couple of times. "We're meeting my *TRAINER*."

"You must come here a lot," Sam said to Dave as Tammy poured the coffee. He eyed the sausage Melinda was frying and said, "I'll take one of those sausage and egg paninis you're making."

Dave chuckled, winked at the ladies and said, "This place has the best coffee in the world. So I meet my friends here pretty regularly. Like I said, it's my favorite morning spot."

From the back corner, a man waved Dave over and they walked toward him. The man stood as they approached, smiled and shook hands with them. He looked like an upside down pyramid—broad shoulders, narrow waist—Sam recognized this man certainly was a *TRAINER*. He must work for a gym.

"Nice to meet you, Sam. Dave has told me about your trouble and I have no doubt we *CAN* help."

"That makes one of us," Sam replied, trying to fake a smile so he would appear to be joking. Neither of the other two laughed and Sam flopped onto his chair feeling more and more like a failure in the presence of two truly disciplined successes.

They chit-chatted for a while and Sam found out quickly the *TRAINER* did not work for the nearby gym; he owned it. Sam felt a little self-conscious about his panini after finding that out, but not enough to stop eating while they talked.

Then Dave said, "Well guys, I think it's time you two got to work. Deborah and I plan to visit her mother today. Sam, I'm going to leave you with my *TRAINER*. He'll get you home when he's done with you.

"Don't worry, he and I'll get together next week to deal with my business. Listen well."

Dave took a final swig from his coffee cup and left Sam sitting there totally nonplussed.

The *TRAINER* smiled and said, "You better finish yours too, we're heading out." Sam drained his cup, asked the barista for a refill in a to-go cup and followed the *TRAINER* out to his truck asking, "Where're we going?"

"To my gym. We're going to start your *TRAINING*."

"I didn't think this was about exercise."

"It's not, but if we sit around and talk in there all day, I'll end up eating more of those paninis and need the exercise like you."

"Great," said Sam sardonically, rolling his eyes.

*****

After a short drive to the gym. They walked into the *TRAINER'S* office. While the *TRAINER* walked around his desk, Sam sat down and said, "Alright, so what is all this *COULDA, SHOULDA, WOULDA* stuff? It sounded weird to begin with and the more I've thought about it, the more it sounds like gobbledy-gook. Do you really think you can help?"

"You wouldn't be here if I didn't. I'm not going to talk about the *SHOULDA* and *WOULDA* 'stuff,' as you call it. That's for Dave's other friends to discuss. I'm just the *TRAINER*. My job is getting you from *COULDA* to *CAN*. I understand your cynicism. I was just like you once. Dave, however, took me under his wing and passed his inheritance on to me."

"Dave helped you?" Sam responded. "I thought you helped Dave."

"We help each other. Dave has seen I'm really good at going from *COULDA* to *CAN*. I help him keep doing it even on days when he doesn't feel like it. That's my job, getting you to *CAN*."

"Well, I guess that's the problem right now," Sam mumbled. "I am beginning to think I can't really do anything. There are so many possibilities out there I *COULD* follow *BUT* I don't know which to choose. And I don't really know if I *CAN* actually do any of them."

Sam was leaning forward in his chair, "I even thought about starting," he paused slouched back in his chair and continued, "never mind. What have you got for me?"

"Sam, your statements actually cut right to the heart of what I want to tell you. Listen carefully. I only have one lesson for you. After that, I *CAN* help keep you going, but it will be up to you to apply the lesson."

"Alright, give it to me," Sam said, pulling out a pen and opening his planner to a notes page.

"The lesson is right here," the *TRAINER* said, pointing to a plaque above his head on the wall behind him. Sam read:

You *can* do
ANYTHINGG

Sam laughed, "If it's such an important lesson, you think you could have spelled it right."

The *TRAINER* smiled indulgently and went on. "Here is what I had to learn a long time ago, Sam. You can't do everything. But you *CAN* do *ANYTHINGG*."

"Is that with two Gs?" Sam asked mockingly.

"Yes, it is, and let me show you why." He handed Sam a card:

31

> You can't do EVERYTHING,
> But you *CAN* do ***ANYTHINGG*!
>
> **A** TTITUDE
>
> **N** EXT STEP THINKING
>
> **Y** OUR STRENGTHS
>
> **T** IME
>
> **H** ONESTY
>
> **I** NSIGHT
>
> **N** EVER QUIT
>
> **G** ROWTH
>
> **G** OALS

"These are the nine keys for getting from *COULDA* to *CAN*.

"Let me explain them.

"*ATTITUDE* is pretty straightforward. I imagine a veteran sales rep like you has taught this lesson over and over again. I also imagine you know as well as I do that it's a load of pop psychology to claim you *CAN* do anything you think you *CAN*. I don't want you to think I am telling you to Positive Mental Attitude your way into success at anything. You can have all the PMA you want, but you'll never swim your way across the Atlantic Ocean by yourself. However, if you already think you can't, there is no way you ever will. Having a positive attitude doesn't get the whole job done, though it gets you a good way down the road. Having a negative one, however,

> "If you already think you can't, there is no way you ever will."

puts the job in the grave. Of course, that may be the reason you and I will never swim across the Atlantic Ocean.

"One of the best ways to work on our *ATTITUDE* is to work on how we speak to ourselves and how we speak about ourselves. People come into my gym overweight and unhealthy. The first thing I try to help them change is their *ATTITUDE.*

"They have to believe they are healthy people or everything I teach them will be an uphill battle. They have to see themselves as exercisers and healthy eaters. Otherwise all they ever see is an overweight, unhealthy person trying to conform to someone else's rigid plan. They may stick to it for a while, however, it's never internalized. They won't maintain it over the long haul.

"What is your *ATTITUDE* Sam?"

"Right now," Sam responded, "It's pretty crummy. I've been told over and over again that I'm too old to fit in the modern companies and sales forces. I am starting to believe it."

"You need to start here, Sam. You need to work on your *ATTITUDE*. You need to envision yourself already accomplishing your goals. You need to speak about yourself with positives and not negatives. You need to list what you are and what you *CAN* do and repeat those things to yourself. I'm going to give you a series of cards to work on each step of my *CAN* lesson. I hope you will go home and work through each of these. They are very simple, asking a few questions to help you think about each step of *ANYTHINGG*."

The *TRAINER* handed Sam a card:

ATTITUDE

Do you usually speak to or about yourself with positives or negatives?

If negative, write the things below and then cross through them, committing yourself to re-move them from your speech.

Turn those negatives into positives and list them below. Commit to telling yourself these things every day.

List some affirmation statements that line up with your goals and dreams. They should begin with "I am..." or "I *CAN*..."

"*NEXT STEP THINKING* simply means you need to be thinking ahead. Too often, people fail because they never think past what they are doing right now. Perhaps I should have called this *LAST STEP THINKING*. But if you think it is funny saying you *CAN* do *ANY-THINGG* with two Gs, imagine what people would say if the card read, 'You can't do *EVE-RYTHING*. But you *CAN* do *ALYTHINGG*.'

"Anyway, you can only get from *COULDA* to *CAN* when you plan. Where do you want your plans to end up? What will it take each step of the way? Think about it this way, Sam. Not that I'm big into borrowing money, but let's say you were thinking of starting a business and were heading to the bank for a small business loan. What would you need to give them?"

"A business plan, I guess."

> "You only *CAN* when you *PLAN*."

"That's right. Why? Because the bank understands this one fact— you only *CAN* when you plan.

"This key is true whether you are talking about a project at work or home or about your life as a whole. I have to think like this in my work as a *TRAINER*. I have to ask people what they see as the end product. Are they here to be more healthy? Are they here to lose weight? Are they here to increase strength? Are they here to bulk up and look muscular? I have to plan their training around what they see as the end result. Then we have to establish a plan to get there."

Sam interrupted, "I understand this. It's just like the company I used to work for. Every year we had these planning meetings. The first step was to determine how the company should look at the end of 10 years. Then 5 years. Then we came down to this year. Where did the company need to be at the end of this year in order to be on our way to the 5 and 10 year plan? Then we broke it into the steps each department needed to take to get to this year's goals."

"That's it exactly, Sam. I knew you already knew this stuff. You just have to apply it to your life as well as your company. Take a look at this card."

NEXT STEP THINKING

Whether you are thinking about your life in general or a particular project, what do you want the end result to look like?

Break that long-term goal into parts. What steps must you take to reach that goal?

What resources do you need? What must you do to get these resources?

What things must you do every year, month, week or day to reach the goal?

What step must you take today to reach the goal?

"*YOUR STRENGTHS* means you *SHOULDN'T* spend your time trying to be someone else. Of course, I have to be careful here. I don't want to jump ahead and get into the *PROFESSOR'S* territory."

"Who's the *PROFESSOR*?" Sam interrupted.

"You'll meet her later," replied the *TRAINER*. "She'll help you get from *SHOULDA* to *SHALL*. Right now, let's suffice it to say you *CAN* only do what *you CAN* do. There is no need to try to do what someone else *CAN* do, even if that someone is your hero. In other words, just because you and I really like Dave, doesn't mean we should start trying to run restaurants. Think about what you're good at and realize the world needs people like you.

"My dad was good at fixing mechanical things. My brother inherited that strength and I didn't. I never understood why on earth they liked working on heating and air conditioning units every day. I tried doing that sort of thing with them for a while, but it's just not my cup of tea. We were all frustrated during that time. I now understand they like doing that because it's their strength. It's who they are. But it's not who I am. Now, when my air conditioner breaks, my plumbing leaks or my lawnmower quits working, I call my brother."

Sam started laughing, remembering his old job, "I know just what you're talking about. It used to frustrate me so badly when my superiors wanted to promote someone for doing a good job and all they thought about was that people in my sales division made more money. They would promote someone who *COULDN'T* sell a coat to a naked Alaskan and wondered why sales went down."

"That's exactly the point," the *TRAINER* said, happy that Sam was starting to see the benefit in all he was telling him.

He handed him the next card. Sam glanced at it quickly.

YOUR STRENGTHS

What are you good at?

With what do others seem to be most impressed about you and your work?

What do you do that produces your greatest re-sults?

What do you do that provides you the greatest satisfaction?

"*TIME* is the reason you cannot do everything. You can probably do a lot more than you realize, but the fact is we only get 24 hours in a day, 7 days in a week, 52 weeks a year. Plus, we are all going to die.

> "Time is like money. You can do four things with it. You can waste it, spend it, invest it or borrow it."

Whether we like it or not, our *TIME* is limited and uncertain. That means each day needs to be used to accomplish what really matters.

"*TIME* is like money. You can do four things with it. You can waste it, spend it, invest it or borrow it. We waste *TIME* when we do useless things that accomplish nothing. We spend it when we do something that provides a benefit now, but that's it. We invest it when we do what is most important, providing benefit not only for the moment but for time to come. Most of us borrow too much *TIME*. When we waste *TIME*, not following through on today's steps to reach the goal, we borrow *TIME* from the

> "Procrastination is the credit card of time. Regrettably, like money, some of us borrow so much time from our future we never catch up."

future. Obligating tomorrow to do today's

work. We call this procrastination. Procrastination is the credit card of time. Regrettably, like money, some of us borrow so much time from our future we never catch up.

"The point is we need to use *TIME* wisely. Benjamin Franklin pointed out that *TIME* is the stuff our lives are made of. If we're just killing *TIME*, we might as well be killing ourselves. You only get to *CAN* when you invest your *TIME* wisely.

"Finally, we do have to realize the only time we actually have is today. You, me and everybody we know only lives one day at a time. Some folks use their one day at a time positively. Some don't. Have you ever caught yourself saying you were going to start a diet tomorrow so just for today, you are going to have that last hurrah and pig out one final time."

Sam's face brightened a few shades of pink. "Yeah, actually come to think about it. I've done that almost every week since I lost my job."

"You see, Sam," the *TRAINER* went on, "that's living your one day at a time in a negative way. You are destroying your health one day at a time. But you can reverse that. Instead of thinking, 'I have to eat healthy for the rest of my life,' think, 'Just for today, I'm going to eat healthy. Tomorrow is a different story, but today, I'll eat healthy.' You obviously won't make any major health strides in just one day. But when you start living one day at a time in a healthy way, you'll be amazed at the results down the road. What's even better is when you have bad days, you don't have to beat yourself up. Instead of lapsing because you had a bad day yesterday, just remember that day is already gone. Who knows what you may do tomorrow, but for today, for the time you have right now, you will make a healthy choice."

The *TRAINER* fell silent for a moment and then said, "Sam, that's powerful stuff I just shared with you and it's not just about your health. It's about your work, your dreams, your family, your relationship with your wife and kids. While you certainly think about and plan for the *NEXT STEP* you have to live in the only time you've got—today."

Sam was wide-eyed, thinking about the number of times he had goofed off "just for to-day" or put off "just for today." He thought about all the days he hadn't spent time with his kids and all the conversations he never had with his wife. "That is powerful," he finally said. "Thank you."

"Here you go," the *TRAINER* said, "Check out this card."

TIME

How much time do you have to accomplish your goals?

Go back to your *NEXT STEP THINKING* and consider the time it will take to accomplish each step. Schedule your steps below and then put them onto your calendar or day planner.

Follow through. Don't borrow *TIME* from tomorrow to accomplish what you planned for today.

"*HONESTY* means looking at all of the things we have already discussed truthfully. Did you ever see *Napolean Dynamite*?"

Sam rolled his eyes. "Yeah, I saw it. My kids love it. I don't get it."

"Yeah, well," the *TRAINER* chuckled, "you either love it or hate it. Anyway, you remember Uncle Rico, who spent the whole movie fantasizing about going back to his high school football championship. He was certain if his coach had put him in as quarterback, they would have won and he would have gone pro and live in a big house with his soul mate."

"That was the one funny part of the movie to me," Sam replied joining in with his own laughter.

The *TRAINER* replied, "Sadly, that was so funny because it describes reality for too many people. A lot of people get to our age, Sam, and think about what they *COULDA* done back when they graduated high school and college *BUT* something got in the way. Usually, they overestimate their youthful abilities. You would be amazed at the number of guys in my gym who know for certain they *COULDA* played pro football if only this or that. One or two of them might be telling the truth. For them, it is sad they didn't go from *COULDA* to *CAN* back then and follow their dreams. Too often they let someone else's expectations or plans for them take over their lives. Now they live with regret. For the rest, what is really sad is they're still living in some fantasy world.

"You have to be *HONEST* about your *ATTITUDE* and learn to tell when it is holding you back. You have to be *HONEST* about your *NEXT STEP THINKING*. That is, you need to be *HONEST* about what obstacles will be in your way and plan for them. You have to be *HONEST* about *YOUR STRENGTHS*. Let's face it Sam, even if you could have gone pro back in the day, you're not going to be doing that now. You need to be *HONEST* about *TIME*. That is why so many people procrastinate. They don't feel like doing anything right now, therefore they put things off. The problem is they're not *HONEST* with themselves about what they really *CAN* do tomorrow. Be *HONEST* with yourself and with everyone else about all of these things. Otherwise you'll waste your time chasing pipe dreams and ten years from now you'll still be talking about all the things you *COULDA* done today *BUT*…"

The *TRAINER* paused for effect and allowed this last statement to sink in and then said, "One of the best ways to be *HONEST* is to ask others. This is tough because they may not want to be *HONEST* with us and we may not want to listen *HONESTLY*. After all, the truth hurts sometimes. If you had a job, I would tell you to talk to your boss or co-workers. You're married with children, therefore a good place to start is with your wife and kids. You will be amazed how much *INSIGHT* they have into where you are with all of the issues we have discussed."

> "One of the best ways to be *HONEST* is to ask others."

HONESTY

For each question, write your own answers and then ask someone else for their input.

Is your *ATTITUDE* holding you back or helping you? How?

How well are you following your *NEXT STEP THINKING* plan?

What really are *YOUR STRENGTHS* and how well are you using them?

How well do you manage your *TIME*?

"*INSIGHT* means relying on what you know. A lot of people think *INSIGHT* is a rare gift. That's not true. *INSIGHT* is simply relying on what a person has learned through a long period of observation, study and experience. They have worked at something for a long time; it only appears to come naturally to everyone else. Let's go back to what you said about people getting promoted into your sales department. How long did it take you to know if they were going to do well there?"

Sam paused for a moment because he did not want to seem haughty, and then replied, "For most of them, I could tell within the first week. I mean, I've been in sales for more than 20 years. I oughta know."

"Exactly," the *TRAINER* replied. "Here's the key you have to understand. A lot of the time, the things you think you can't do are simply things you don't have *INSIGHT* about. You haven't observed them, studied them or experienced them. If there is something you want to do, you have to study what it takes to do it, observe those who are doing it and then jump in and experience it. Of course, that means you're going to make mistakes. But as you learn from those mistakes, you gain *INSIGHT* that gets you to *CAN*."

"I've got *INSIGHT* in sales and that's about it. What happens if I can't get another job in sales?"

"You might get another job in sales. But then again you might have to change fields if you get another job. One of the best steps you *CAN* take is to start studying the field, get to know people who are in the field and observe them. Then, when you applied for the job you would have *INSIGHT* to offer. Whatever choices you make you have to devote the *TIME* to study, observe and experience the work you want to do, gaining *INSIGHT*. Some have suggested if you spent one hour a day, at least five days a week, studying and observing the field or work in which you are interested, you will become an expert in six months to a year. Are you willing to invest that *TIME*? Check out this card."

INSIGHT

What have you already studied, observed and experienced? How can your *INSIGHT* serve you to reach your goals?

In what areas do you need to have *INSIGHT* to accomplish your goals?

What can you study? Who can you observe? How can you experience the work in which you want to have *INSIGHT*?

Schedule the *TIME* needed to gain your new *INSIGHT*.

"*NEVER QUIT* is important at this point because gaining *INSIGHT* through experience kills many attempts at getting to *CAN*. I'm sure Dave has mentioned he started his first restaurant at 25."

"Yeah, he mentioned that," Sam said, eager to hear a little more about Dave's success.

"Has he told you he nearly went bankrupt in his first attempt?"

"What?!" Sam exclaimed, nearly falling over in the chair he had been leaning back on two legs.

"Oh yeah. He usually waits and lets me tell people about that. Dave knew he wanted to get into the restaurant business. When he was a kid, he had a good friend whose dad owned a restaurant. His friend's dad always seemed to be having fun. That's what Dave wanted. However, back then, Dave didn't know anything about managing a restaurant, picking the right people to work in a restaurant or leading the people he had working for him. He made a series of bad choices that put him on the brink of bankruptcy.

"About ready to throw in the towel, he went to his friend's dad and wanted to know what he was doing wrong. He was told, 'You're not learning from your mistakes. Hang in there. Pay attention to what is working and what is not. You'll gain the *INSIGHT* you need to make it.' Dave decided to stick with it. He was certain about success and he decided he was not going to quit, no matter what. In a couple of years, he was running one of the most successful independent restaurants in town.

"What would have happened if he quit while he was still gaining *INSIGHT*? Who knows? Hopefully he would be sitting where you are, learning from someone about how he should *NEVER QUIT*.

"I think you will like this card. There is not much work to it."

NEVER

QUIT!

"*GROWTH* is just that. You have got to *GROW*. In a very real sense, there are things you *CAN* do that you can't do today. However, if you *NEVER QUIT* while you gain *INSIGHT*, *YOUR STRENGTHS* will grow and you will do more than you ever thought possible.

"I train a lot of people in this gym. Many of them come in with a secret desire to be Arnold Schwarzenegger. Most of them *CAN*. It won't be today, tomorrow or even this year. However, if they keep up their *NEXT STEP THINKING* and *NEVER QUIT* they will get there. They have to be willing to *GROW* slowly, step by step. That *GROWTH* is not necessarily easy. It means pushing and challenging themselves with each workout. It means reaching a *GOAL* but not stopping. However, in time, everyone who works to *GROW* makes progress. Measure that progress and you will be pushed to *GROW* even more.

"Face it, Sam, you're not going to be in Dave's financial shoes by this time next year. However, if you're willing to *GROW*, you'll get there…eventually. Are you willing to *GROW?* Use this card to help."

GROWTH

Where are you right now regarding the skills needed to accomplish your goals?

In what do you need to grow to accomplish your goals?

How can you measure your growth?

Looking back, what growth have you already accomplished in these areas?

"*GOALS* is the final key. I know, you are thinking this could have been put under *NEXT STEP THINKING* and then I wouldn't have misspelled my key word. However, this point is not about planning. It brings us full circle to *ATTITUDE*. Let's face it. We all feel better when we have victories under our belt. If you want some really practical advice on moving from *COULDA* to *CAN*, set attainable intermediary *GOALS*. Then celebrate each one.

> "If you want some really practical advice on moving from *COULDA* to *CAN*, set yourself some attainable intermediary *GOALS*. Then celebrate each one you accomplish."

"I started my daughter running when she was eight. She hated it until we got into our first race. Some runners, who are much better than me, run in those races to win. I run for the experience. However, as you can imagine, there were not many kids in the 10 and under bracket for a 5k Turkey Trot. Winning that medal changed my daughter's outlook on running completely. Today, she *CAN* run better than me. Why? Because she was rewarded for accomplishing a *GOAL*. Take this last card. It's simple, but it's necessary."

GOALS

What are the intermediary goals on your way to
your big goal?

How will you celebrate reaching these goals?

With whom will you celebrate them?

"That's it, Sam."

"That's it? You say that like I've been sitting here for only ten minutes. This all makes sense. I mean, really, I kind of already knew all of it. Seeing it laid out like this really helps. But, I gotta tell you, it's pretty weighty stuff. It's going to take me forever to get it all down and I'm not sure I even can."

"Let me be *HONEST* with you. Getting it completely right will take you a lifetime. After all, it is about *GROWTH*. We are like trees, Sam. If we stop *GROWING*, we've died. I don't get it right all the time. Dave doesn't get it right all the time. That's why we help each other. That's why we're here to help you. And that's why we'll eventually rely on you to help us. The point is, Sam, you *CAN* start the journey from *COULDA* to *CAN* today and each day you *WILL* get better.

"Now, let's go grab a bite of lunch and get to know one another a little better. I'll let you mull over what we've talked about today on your own. Take some time this week to work through the cards I gave you. I know Dave will want to get together with you again soon to see what you thought of all this."

"Great, I'm starved," said Sam gathering up the cards and his notes.

Sam looked at the summary card one more time before he put it into his planner.

> You can't do EVERYTHING,
> But you *CAN* do ***ANYTHINGG!***
>
> **A**TTITUDE
>
> **N**EXT STEP THINKING
>
> **Y**OUR STRENGTHS
>
> **T**IME
>
> **H**ONESTY
>
> **I**NSIGHT
>
> **N**EVER QUIT
>
> **G**ROWTH
>
> **G**OALS

*****

Sam showed Susan the cards when he got home and told her what the *TRAINER* had taught him about the nine keys of getting from *COULDA* to *CAN*. She thought it sounded neat but added, "I sure hope this isn't going to stop you from looking for a job. It seems to me you *SHOULD* get a job first, then you *CAN* start looking at all this stuff."

"I don't know, Susan. You know I've thought about starting a landscaping business..."

"Yeah, *BUT* honey," Susan interrupted, "like you've always said, if you start working for yourself, you lose all those great employee benefits."

"Well, look at where those benefits have gotten me. I don't know," Sam said thoughtfully, "You might be right. I'll wait and see if Dave calls me again. I think he has another friend he wants me to see. Somebody called the *PROFESSOR*. That really sounds weird. Either way, I'll hit the classifieds and call my recruiter again tomorrow."

*****

A week later, Dave called Sam.

"I'm sorry Dave," Sam stammered, "I've been meaning to call you, but I'm just overwhelmed looking for a job."

"That's okay, Sam," Dave replied. "Most people I've worked with are overwhelmed by the *TRAINER*."

Sam was taken aback by Dave's perception. "Well, I was overwhelmed with that too. However, I have to admit I have been thinking about some plans, you know *NEXT STEP THINKING*. I just don't know if I should try this 'start my own business' thing, I mean, it's so iffy and the benefits I would be losing…"

"Losing, Sam? What benefits do you have right now?"

"You know what I mean, Dave. I have to think about my family. Like I said, I probably *SHOULD* just look for another secure job."

"I'll tell you what, Sam. Let's not discuss what you *SHOULD* do until we meet with one of my other friends tomorrow. You know the drill. I'll meet you at 5:45 in my driveway."

"Is this the *PROFESSOR*?"

"Yes, that's what we call her."

"What's that all about?"

"Meet me at 5:45 and you'll find out."

The PROFFESOR

From SHOULDA to SHALL

Sam had little trouble getting up this time. He still wasn't sure about all this *GETTING TO DID* business. However, he was intrigued enough by his meeting with the *TRAINER* that he really didn't want to miss meeting the *PROFESSOR*.

At 5:44 he walked up Dave's driveway, slid into the car and said, "Are we going to *The Early Bird* again?"

"Oh yeah," Dave replied. "I don't drink coffee anyplace else, especially if I'm paying."

After a few moments, Dave continued, "So, did you learn anything from the *TRAINER*?"

"I don't know," Sam said after a brief hesitation. "The *ANYTHINGG* stuff was neat and I think it *CAN* work. *BUT*, like I told the *TRAINER*, everything is so iffy. Susan thinks I *SHOULD* get a job first and then talk with you more about this stuff. She's afraid I'm going to follow some hare-brained scheme and try going into business for myself, *BUT* then I won't have any benefits, no retirement package. You know the story."

Dave smiled indulgently.

"I'm just not sure what I *SHOULD* do at this point. I mean, my dad always said I *SHOULD* think about my family first. Having a good, steady job seems to be what is best for them. I gotta tell you though," Sam continued, this time with a slight gleam of excitement, "the idea of going out on my own really gets my blood pumping. Especially after getting slapped by my good, steady job. One thing is for certain, if I'm working for me, I'll never get fired again."

Dave laughed along with Sam at this as they pulled into the coffee shop parking lot. When they walked in, the aroma of espresso mingled with that of frying eggs and bacon; Sam began to lick his lips. Tammy said, "Hey

Dave." Melinda looked up and, seeing Sam, said, "Another panini?"

Sam looked around to make sure he didn't see the *TRAINER* anywhere and said, "Bring it on."

Sam and Dave walked to the same table in the back of the café. This time a sharply dressed woman, who looked as though she could have only just recently become a grandmother, greeted them with a smile and a handshake.

Dave said, "Sam, I would like you to meet my *PROFESSOR. PROFESSOR*, this is Sam."

"Alright," blurted Sam, "I imagine Dave wants to shoot the breeze for a few minutes and then leave me stranded here with you. He probably doesn't want me asking a bunch of questions yet. But I have to know why you're called the *PROFESSOR*. I mean, it sounds a little too 'Gilligan's Island' for me."

"I'm called the *PROFESSOR*," she respond-ed looking as though she didn't quite appre-ciate Sam's humor, "because that is what I am, or that is what I was. I am now the Presi-dent of our nearby university. But I still teach. Would you prefer that I were the *MOVIE STAR*?"

Sam tried to smile but was slightly ab-ashed, then both Dave and the *PROFESSOR* burst out laughing. Sam didn't know quite what to make of this. Despite the humor, to Sam, the *PROFESSOR* at least looked the part. She was impeccably dressed. She sat up like she had a board up the back of her shirt. Every hair was in place. She looked like she had never dangled a participle a day in her life, whatever that means, Sam thought.

"Well," said Dave, "that's the first time anyone ever brought up 'Gilligan's Island.' Maybe I should try to add a movie star into our retinue. I always liked Maryann better though. Either way, like Sam said, I am going to strand you two together. I'm taking a three-hour tour of a couple of my restaurants today, plus I'm checking out a possible buy on a small apartment complex. What do you think I *SHOULD* do about that, *PROFESSOR*?"

Before the *PROFESSOR* could respond with more than a reproving look, Dave said, "I'm only joking. You can talk to Sam about the *SHOULDAS* today. I'll catch up with both of you later this week."

Then draining his coffee and ordering a blueberry muffin to go, Dave walked out whistling.

"As soon as you're done with your sandwich," the *PROFESSOR* said, "we'll head to the school. I'm keeping office hours today and prefer to be on campus."

Sam finished up and once again asked for more coffee in a to-go cup. Melinda said, "Keep hanging out with Dave and his friends and you'll be a regular too."

"I certainly understand why Dave is," Sam said. "Does he own this café?"

"Oh no," Melinda replied, "I own this. Dave encouraged me with his *GETTING TO DID* business, but this puppy is all mine."

Sam was impressed as he walked out sipping his delicious coffee. Maybe Dave and his friends could help. As he left, Tammy mumbled something to Melinda. "What was that?" Sam said expectantly.

"Oh nothing," Tammy replied with a mischievous grin. "We'll see you next week, if not sooner."

The *PROFESSOR* chuckled as they walked out and got in her car.

*****

Sam followed the *PROFESSOR* into an extremely wooden office. The dark leather furniture even seemed to blend into the wood-grained walls. Instead of sitting behind her desk, the *PROFESSOR* picked up her phone and said, "Helen, I'm in a *PRIORITY* meeting." After a brief pause, "Thank you." Then, after putting the phone down, she sat in a wing-backed recliner, crossed her legs and offered Sam a seat on the divan on the other side of the coffee table.

"A *PRIORITY* meeting?" Sam questioned.

"That's a code word between my staff and me. *PRIORITY* meeting means two things."

"And what are those?" Sam asked, certain he was about to learn some amazing secret about conducting meetings.

"First, I only want emergency calls and calls from my husband, kids or grandkids sent through. And second...," she paused seeing Sam's expectant look, "keep the coffee coming. I don't want to be distracted by getting it myself." The *PROFESSOR* chuckled at Sam's bewilderment.

As if on cue, Helen walked in with two mugs and a thermal carafe of coffee. "Tammy and Melinda roasted these beans yesterday," Helen noted with a smile before leaving.

"Great," the *PROFESSOR* said and then turned to Sam. "Alright, let's get down to business. The *TRAINER'S* job was to get you from

COULDA to *CAN.* My job is to get you from *SHOULDA* to *SHALL.*"

"What on earth does that mean?" Sam interjected.

"Be patient, Sam. By the time I'm done, you'll understand. Have you noticed the picture behind my desk?"

Sam looked at the portrait as he took a sip of coffee. It showed two men. Both reminded him somewhat of the *TRAINER*, though both were clearly dressed in some sort of ancient toga type garb. One of the men was laughing, holding a basket full of golden apples and walking away from the other who looked as though he were yelling angry epithets. This second one was stooped, every muscle was bulging under the weight of the entire earth on his shoulders.

"That's how I feel sometimes," Sam muttered. "What's it all about?"

"For me," the *PROFESSOR* responded, "it represents a lot of things. However, it is an artist's depiction of Atlas and Hercules. Have you heard the story?"

Sam shook his head; so the *PROFESSOR* continued, "According to myth, Hercules was given 12 mammoth tasks by the king of Mycenae. The eleventh was to retrieve golden apples from the Hesperides. I could spend all day talking about this, but if you want to know more about the Hesperides, their apples and why this was such a big task, look it up on the internet. Hercules knew only one person who could get the Hesperides to give up any of their golden apples—their father, Atlas.

"Hercules hit a snag here—Atlas was busy. Having been punished by Zeus, he was condemned to carry the weight of the heavens on his shoulder. Hercules visited Atlas and offered to give him a break from holding up the heavens, if he would get some of his daughters' apples. Atlas agreed and got the apples. However, when he returned he told Hercules he was not going to take back the weight of the heavens.

"There stood Hercules bearing the crushing weight of the heavens. Instead of getting mad at Atlas, he had planned for just such an event. He shrugged and in essence said, 'I can't blame you. I guess you got the better of me on this one, Atlas. Well, if I'm going to have to carry this weight, I might as well get comfortable. Could you help me adjust the padding on my shoulder?' When Atlas lifted the heavens to help Hercules adjust his toga, Hercules stepped out from under the heavens and let them fall squarely on Atlas' shoulders. He then picked up the basket of apples and took them back to the king of Mycenae."

"That's a great story," Sam said without much conviction in his voice, "but what's your point? Don't be stupid like Atlas?"

"Actually, yes. A lot of us today are, as you put it, 'stupid like Atlas.' When you first saw the picture, you said it was how you feel sometimes. What did you mean?"

Sam didn't have to think about his reply this time, "Right now I feel like I have the weight of the whole world on my shoulders. I think about all that my dad told me I *SHOULD* do to provide for my family. I think about what Susan, my wife, keeps telling me I *SHOULD* do. I think about what Dave tells me I *SHOULD* do. I think about what the *TRAINER* said I *SHOULD* do. Now I'm going to have to think about what you say I *SHOULD* do. Not to mention everything that is expected from what our society and my church says I *SHOULD* do. It gets to be a bit overwhelming, almost paralyzing.

"I'm like that guy in the picture, Atlas. I'm being crushed by the weight of the world. I can't figure out which way I *SHOULD* go and I just want to scream at the people who seem to be only carrying apples."

"That, Sam, is exactly how I felt several years ago, back when I still lived next door to Dave."

"You lived next door to Dave? That's where I live."

"I know, I hope you don't think we asked too much for that house," the *PROFESSOR* said laughing.

Sam looked again at the name plate on the huge cherry desk and suddenly realized why the *PROFESSOR'S* name had seemed so familiar. He had signed what seemed like a thousand papers with her and her husband's signatures already on them. He chuckled.

"No. We thought the price was great. We just hope we get to keep living there by the time I get through all this."

The *PROFESSOR* smiled and said, "Me too. Back to Atlas and Hercules; and you and me. As I said a few minutes ago, many of us are stupid like Atlas and let the rest of the world put their weight on our shoulders. Too many of us are carrying the weight of the world on our *SHOULD*-ers.

"We keep hearing what we *SHOULD* do from everyone in our families, churches, neighborhoods, companies, schools and so on. Not to mention all the *SHOULDAS* we tell ourselves every day. Then after years of living in the world of *SHOULDA*, we look around and see we are not where we want to be. Or worse, we follow all the *SHOULDAS* and our world falls apart anyway, like when you lose the job from which you thought you would retire. Then we spend our time telling everyone who will listen how our lives *COULDA* been better because we *SHOULDA* done this or that, *BUT* one thing or another got in the way. After years of that, we develop a phenomenally big *BUT*. I want to help you get rid of that big *BUT* by helping you get that weight off your *SHOULD*-ers. We need to remove all the useless *SHOULDAS* and turn the profitable ones into *SHALLS*."

"How do you do that?" Sam asked sitting up a little taller, expecting to get to some real wisdom.

"In the big picture, there are really only three profitable *SHOULDAS*."

The *PROFESSOR* got up and retrieved a business card from her desk. As she sat back down, she handed the card to Sam. He examined it closely:

Your 3 "You Shalls"

You SHALL be the best You

You SHALL go beyond Yourself

You SHALL Prioritize

"I *SHALL*?" Sam inquired nonplussed.

"You *SHALL*," the *PROFESSOR* responded with confidence. "Remember, my job is to help you turn your *SHOULDAS* into *SHALLS*. These are the three things you *SHOULDA* do. If you are wise, they are the three things you *SHALL* do."

"Well, this ought to be easier than what the *TRAINER* taught me. He had nine things. But what do they mean?" objected Sam.

"'*You SHALL be the best You*' means you *SHOULD* not try to be someone else. You *SHOULD* not try to be your parents or your siblings. You *SHOULD* not try to be your spouse, your neighbors or your boss. You *SHALL* be the very best you you can be.

"Too many people are busy trying to be someone else. They see a personality they like, usually one opposite to their own, and try to be that person. It never works. Some want to please the people in their lives, so they try to follow all the advice every-

> "Too many people are busy trying to be someone else. They see a personality they like, usually one opposite to their own, and try to be that person. It never works."

one else tells them they *SHOULD* follow. Our parents told us where we *SHOULD* go to school, what kind of career we *SHOULD* have and even what kind of person we *SHOULD* marry. Don't get me wrong, a great deal of the time our parents give us great advice, after all, at that time in our lives they are a lot smarter than we are. However, in the end we have to be the best us. We are the ones who have to live with our education, our career and most especially our spouse.

"In addition to parents, teachers told us what we *SHOULD* major in at college. Our friends tell us what we *SHOULD* do every step of the way. However, each person's perspective is colored by their own outlook. And each person is different. I hope you understand what we are talking about here. Obviously, I believe there is right and wrong. I believe there are moral guidelines everyone *SHOULD* follow. I am not talking about this as though each person is free to make up their own morality. That discussion, however, is for the preacher, not the *PROFESSOR*. That is not what we are focusing on in *GETTING TO DID*. We are talking about the general path of your life.

"You must learn to be you. Don't even try to be Dave. I know Dave is encouraging you to start your own business. Perhaps you *SHOULD*. But if you *SHOULD*, it is not because Dave says so. As I'm sure you can tell, I don't own this university. I work for it. I'm right where I *SHOULD* be and even Dave knows that. Whatever choices you make about your new career, let it be you coming through."

Sam sighed. "That's interesting. I have felt the weight on my *SHOULD*-ers. On the one hand, my wife says I *SHOULD* get a normal job. On the other, although Dave hasn't actually come out and said, 'You *SHOULD* start your own business,' he's certainly implied it dozens of times. Does he know you're telling me not to take his advice?"

"Oh, he knows I am going to tell you to be you and not try to be him. He believes that is better advice than any specific career advice.

Let me put it to you this way. I am a career-minded woman. I balanced raising kids with a job outside the home as well. It wasn't easy; however, I did it. I have always worked to move higher and higher up the ladder until now I am at the top in this university.

"Helen has been the school president's secretary for nearly 20 years. She started after her children left for college. I have a hard time understanding that. She has a hard time understanding the choices I made. We argue about it occasionally. But what we've both learned is she's happy in her role and I'm happy in mine. She has done great things for this school in her role, just as I have. She has done well by her family following her path; I have done well by mine. We did not do everything exactly the same way, but we have both been ourselves. In that regard, I think both of us have been equally successful in life. But don't tell Helen I said that…it would take the fun out of arguing with her about it."

"OK, I'm trying to follow you here," Sam stammered. "I need to be me. That may mean being the university president or it may mean being the president's secretary. That may mean starting my own business or it may mean finding another job. I'm not sure you're helping me out, how do I be me?"

"Yes, well, that is one of those interesting questions to which you would think everyone would know the answer. Yet so often we don't because we have become so blinded by what everyone else expects of us. Here are a few guidelines to help you be you.

"First, *break the molds*. Breaking the molds doesn't necessarily mean wearing wild ties or being an eccentric nut. It does mean you do not have to fit in your parents' or older siblings' molds. Don't try to live in the shoes they filled. Your feet, like your fingerprints, are different from everyone else's. Just because your dad was an accountant, doesn't mean you have to be. Just because your older sister works for the family business, doesn't mean you have to. Just because your father-in-law runs a company, doesn't mean you have to work there.

"Second, *disregard the prophecies* of your parents, professors and peers. You do not have to be what everyone else said you would grow up to be. Did you have class prophecies in high school? You know...the 'Most likely to' statements?"

"Sure we did. I still look back at that yearbook and my picture: 'Most likely to get early parole.' I was always pretty much a troublemaker in high school," Sam chuckled remembering a childhood prank.

82

The *PROFESSOR* smiled and continued, "I was voted 'Most likely to never break a nail.' At the time I thought it was funny. I didn't really have any ambitions. I had not done very well in school. I always joked that I was planning on marrying somebody rich and living off him so it didn't matter. The reality was I didn't think I *COULD* ever really amount to much.

"My parents divorced when I was in elementary school and were, sadly, too often caught up in their own feuding to pay much attention to me. When they did pay attention, it was usually to jump on me about something. The first few years after the divorce were tough and I didn't try in school. My teachers thought I was of no account. Now I know what goes on in those staff rooms and I know my reputation preceded me. They all thought I was a waste of their time.

"This is where God was looking out for me and protected me where I did not protect myself. Most people in my position marry someone just as unhealthy has they are. I, however, met a great man." The *PROFESSOR* nodded to the picture of a handsome man on the bookshelf.

"Hey," Sam exclaimed. "That's the doctor who performed my dad's bypass a few years ago. He was great. Explained what was going on every step of the way. Provided comfort when things looked like they weren't going to go anywhere. He even prayed with us."

The *PROFESSOR* smiled. "Yes, my husband is a great doctor and a wonderful husband and father. For some reason he didn't know about all the prophecies everyone else had for me. He actually thought I *COULD* be some-thing great and filled my head with dreams of a meaningful life. However, to do that, I had to quit thinking of myself in the terms that my parents, peers and professors had always thought of me. I had to forget their prophecies.

"Are you with me so far?"

"Yeah," Sam said, "Break the molds and forget the prophecies. I guess I need to re-member that with my own kids too. My son, Scott, and I have been arguing about where he should go to college. You're saying I *SHOULD* stop forcing Scott down my path."

> "Break the molds and forget the prophecies."

"I'm glad to see you are applying this in-formation to your practical life. Of course, if he wants advice on college, I know a good one he *SHOULD* go to," the *PROFESSOR* smiled, winked and then said in response to Sam's surprised look, "Only kidding, Sam. Continuing on. If you are going to be the best you you can be, the third thing you must do is *work from your strengths*. If you can overlook ending a phrase with a preposition, then I'll tell you to find what you are good at and bank on that. You can't strive for excellence by constantly working where you have no strength. Maybe you should spend some time working on your weaknesses, but spending too much time there typically means you're trying to be someone else. You have clearly been good at sales. That suggests you are a people person. I imagine you like talking to people and hate locking yourself in a room to do detail work. Am I right?"

"Pretty close," Sam smiled.

"If you're good in dealing with people, then make sure whether you start your own business, or find another job, that you do something that connects you to people. You have a Masters degree in accounting, but you certainly *SHOULD* not go find an accounting office to hole yourself up in going over company financial statements all day.

"This is one of the funny things about people. They often spend all of their time thinking about what they *SHOULDA* done when they were younger to be making the big bucks today. They watch a baseball game and think about how they *SHOULDA* stuck with baseball in high school. They watch their favorite actor or actress and think about how they SHOULDA gone to acting school. They listen to their favorite song playing on the radio and think about how they SHOULDA started that band they always dreamed about. How many of these people are really as good as the people who make all those jobs look easy? Not many. There are a lot of people out there who are not any good at baseball, acting or singing who keep trying to pursue those careers because they want to make lots of money. Here is a newsflash, only the ones who are working with their strengths are making any money at it. Think of it this way: you may be a janitor, working night and day dreaming about how you wish you were an actor. It is better, however, to be a good working janitor, than a sorry out of work actor. Find what you are good at, where your strengths are and do that.

"Finally, to be you, *do what you enjoy*. Do that about which you are passionate. Do not settle for a career you are going to hate because you think it is safe and will keep the bills paid. You have already learned finding a safe, secure job is impossible. You might as well do what you enjoy doing. It may fall flat after a few years and everyone will say they told you so, just as you fear they will. Then again, you may opt for another safe, secure job and be at this same point again in 10 years. Why not do what excites you? Why not do what truly motivates you?

"Dave left earlier to go make rounds at his restaurants and consider a possible buy on an apartment complex. On these days, Dave gets up a little earlier because that excites him. If that was all I had to look forward to in my day, I would hit the snooze button a dozen times. But meeting with you here, teaching a dozen college kids, helping other teachers... I live for that. Dave would never make it as a university professor or president, you might not either. But this is exactly where I *SHOULD* be.

"I know I am stepping over into the *COACH'S* realm and I have to be careful, but it is a lot easier to be successful when you are doing what you enjoy. It is a lot easier to be successful when you have that natural motivation.

"Are you keeping up with me so far?"

"I think so," Sam replied. "I *SHALL* be the best me I can possibly be. I *CAN* do that by first breaking the molds and second forgetting the prophecies made for me by others. Then I *SHALL* pursue what I am good at and what I am passionate about."

"Well, that was succinct. As you can tell, I am not any good at brevity," the *PROFESSOR* chuckled. "There is another side to being the best You. You have to remember you can only work on you. You can't make anyone else *GET TO DID*. You are not responsible for managing anyone else's thoughts and feelings. You are merely responsible to be the best you you can be.

"A friend of mine uses a great phrase I now use to remind me what I need to do to be the best me I can possibly be. She always says her job is merely to do the Next Right Thing. No matter how anyone else is acting, no matter how they might react, she wants to do the Next Right Thing. When you make the decision to do the Next Right Thing despite how anyone else is going to act or react, then you are making yourself a better you."

The *PROFESSOR* fell silent for a moment letting this sink in. After a few seconds Sam replied, "So, you're saying even if my wife doesn't like something and starts acting badly about it, I still have to do what's right. I don't get to blame her if I fly off the handle or if I make a mistake because I am responsible to do the Next Right Thing no matter how she acts."

"Sam, I don't know why you think you *CAN*'t do this stuff. You are so far ahead in your thinking than most of the folks Dave brings through here."

"I don't know about all that. But what if I have already botched this? What if I have already flown of the handle or blamed her? What do I do then?"

"That is easy. You apologize and make amends and you do that even if she refuses to apologize for her wrongs. You do the Next Right Thing by owning your part and making it right."

"That's tough. I'll need to work on that one."

The *PROFESSOR* allowed the silence to settle in again to let Sam mull over all she had said so far. Sam took advantage of the Silence to review the bullet points he had made on the note page in his planner.

-You Shall be the Best You

1. Break the molds

2. Disregard the prophecies of others

3. Work from your strengths

4. Do what you enjoy

5. Always do the next right thing

6. Apologize and make amends

After a moment, the *PROFESSOR* continued speaking, "As you know, I'm the *PROFESSOR*, so it shouldn't surprise you that I'm going to give you some homework. For each of the '*You SHALLS*' I have an assignment for you to work through over the next week before you get together with Dave again. Here is the first one."

The *PROFESSOR* handed Sam a sheet of paper.

You SHALL be the best YOU

How are you different from your parents, siblings, spouse, boss, co-workers, etc?

(The world needs people who are just like you. Enjoy these differences.)

What "prophecies" were made about you from your parents, professors and peers? Write them down and mark through them.

(You are more than these prophecies, don't let them limit you.)

What are you good at?

What do you enjoy?

What do you want to do with your life?

"*You SHALL go beyond Yourself.*"

"That sounds odd," Sam interrupted, looking down at the business card again. "It seems to contradict your first statement. First, I'm supposed to be me, now I'm supposed to be more than me? I don't get it."

"Yes," the PROFESSOR replied. "On the surface, they do seem to contradict. However, this statement does not mean we should be more than who we are. Our first SHALL is all about just being ourselves, this one is about thinking about more than ourselves.

"If I might moralize for a moment, I don't think we are here just to get personal fulfillment out of life. Further, I do not think we get personal fulfillment out of life by seeking our own anyway. I do think we are here to add to our world. I do think we are here to help others be more and do more. The greatest fulfillment I have ever had is when I have given of myself to others.

"Have you ever seen the movie *Mr. Holland's Opus*?"

"No," Sam replied.

"Oh that is too bad," the PROFESSOR responded. "I'm giving you another homework assignment, go home and watch that movie. Richard Dreyfuss plays the main character, Mr. Holland. At the beginning of it, he is a young musician planning to be famous. He is already working on a symphony that will make him rich. He takes a teaching job to pay the bills and support his composing until he finally hits the big time. At first, he hates teaching. He cannot stand the kids and, frankly, they can't stand him either. Then his principal rebukes him, pointing out that his job is not just passing on information. It is also providing a compass in life for the kids.

"That starts a change. As the movie continues, he no longer views teaching as a means to get a paycheck so he can do his own thing. Rather, he focuses on the joy of helping the students have breakthroughs. There is more to the movie, but Mr. Holland's journey is one of becoming a servant. When his work as a teacher ceases to be a self-serving way to make money and pay for his real dream and becomes an opportunity to serve others and make a difference, he really begins to write his own magnum opus.

"Toward the end of the movie, Mr. Holland's school hits financial difficulties and cuts his department. He sums up his journey saying, 'It's almost funny. I got dragged into this gig kicking and screaming and now it's the only thing I want to do...'

"I will not ruin the movie for you completely. However, this is what I mean by going beyond yourself. If your life is only ever about you, it will be miserable, no matter how much money you make or how far you go. However, if you go beyond yourself to give to others, helping them be more, you will find fulfillment and meaning in life.

"Why do you think Dave reaches out and gives his time to help people like you and me? He understands this point.

"As you think about what you are going to do and how you are going to approach it, it *SHOULD* not be just about you getting what you want. It *SHOULD* be about you giving to your family and to your community.

"Really, our society is amazing. We went from the 1960's when a president who was considered part of the liberal political party told the nation, 'Ask not what your country can do for you, ask what you can do for your country' to the 1980's when one of the most conservative of the conservatives ran asking the nation the all important question, 'Are you better off than you were four years ago?' We are close to 30 years beyond that now. Some suggest we are riding the pendulum back to a community and service mindset. I hope so. Nevertheless, Sam, if you simply strive to hoard to yourself, your life will be wasted. You *SHALL* go beyond yourself. You *SHALL* shamelessly give yourself to others."

"So, what you're saying is this:" Sam cut in, "if I really want to have a meaningful life and personal fulfillment, I need to give to others."

"Yes and no. If you are only giving to others in order to have personal fulfillment, it will not work. That is manipulation and hypocrisy. No, do not give just to receive. Instead, learn to give of yourself to your family and your community simply for the sake of serving others, treating others the way you want to be treated simply because it is the Next Right Thing. If you do that, then, yes, you will have personal fulfillment and a meaningful life. Do not question me too deeply about it. I do not know why it works. I'm merely certain it does.

"You *SHALL* go beyond yourself by figuring out what your strengths can add to others and to our world. To accomplish this, you have to keep your eyes open. There are opportunities to get beyond ourselves all around us. We just have to be aware. We have to listen. One of the best ways to get beyond yourself is to look around at what bothers you about our world. Then figure out what you can do about it.

"One of the funniest cartoons I have ever seen showed two men sitting at the base of a tree. One says, 'Sometimes I think I might just go ask God why he doesn't do anything about all the bad stuff happening.' The other responded, 'Why don't you?' To which the first replied, 'I'm always afraid he might ask me the same question.'"

Sam and the PROFESSOR both laughed at this. The PROFESSOR continued, "You need to understand one more aspect of getting beyond yourself. What you do doesn't always have to be big. It doesn't have to be on a grand scale. It doesn't have to be about the whole world. It may just be about one person. Do not be paralyzed thinking you cannot do anything about world hunger; find a person to feed. Do not be overwhelmed thinking about all the children who don't have great parents; find a child to whom you can be a great father. It might even just be your own child. This is going beyond yourself."

> "What you do doesn't always have to be big. It doesn't have to be on a grand scale. It doesn't have to be about the whole world. It may just be about one person."

"Ok," Sam wanted to sum up what he had heard so far. "I SHALL be the best me I can be by breaking the mold, forgetting others' prophecies and then pursuing my strengths and my passions, doing the next right thing and apologizing when I blow it. Then I SHALL go beyond myself by using my strengths and my passions to give of myself to others, namely my family and my community."

"That's right," the *PROFESSOR* nodded, pleased Sam was retaining so much. "Here is some more homework for you."

You SHALL go beyond Yourself

Who else does your life immediately impact?

How can your strengths benefit others? …your family?
…your community?

Of what needs are you aware in others? …your family?
…your community? …your world?

What bothers you about your world? What can you do
about it?

Who do you know right now that could use your help?
What will you do to help them?

Sam looked down at the business card and said, "Alright, You Shall be the Best You. You Shall Go Beyond Yourself. Let's look at the third one."

"*You SHALL Prioritize*," the *PROFESSOR* intoned.

"I think I know what this one means," Sam said. "There's only so much *TIME* in a day. Even when I'm being the best me and striving to give of myself to the community, I still can't do everything. I *SHOULD* choose what I'm going to focus on."

"That's exactly right," the *PROFESSOR* said. "Obviously, in any job or in any role you fill, there are some things you have to do because they are your responsibilities and you are not free to delegate them to anyone else. However, beyond those, you need to give careful thought to what you are going to devote your time. This is *PRIORITIZING*. If you over-schedule and over-commit, you will have a lot of irons in the fire, but none of them will be getting hot enough to use."

"How *SHALL* I prioritize?" Sam questioned.

"One great practical test for prioritizing your life is the obituary test. When you die, what would you like written in your obituary? When you figure out what things you would like people to say about you after you're gone, you can start focusing on accomplishing those goals while you're still here. However, the truth of the matter is the issue is really not so much determining what you will do. The issue is determining what you will not do. You can determine what you do by following the first two *SHALLS*. The problem is there will be all kinds of distractions. Not a day will go by that you won't think or hear about some other good work in which you will think you *SHOULD* be involved. You have to learn to say, 'No,' to what is merely good so you can be involved in what is absolutely great. Listen to me on this one, Sam; there are enough people in the world to get everything done. But only if each of us do what is best for us to do.

"Do not get bogged down trying to do other things. If an activity will not help you further your *PRIORITIES*, cut it out. If it is not helping accomplish the goals, it is detrimental to them. That is why I do not get the coffee during *PRIORITY* meetings.

"Become the best you you can be by following your strengths and your passions, then go beyond yourself by giving to your family and community. Then choose the important things you are going to focus on and *PRIORIT-IZE* them by throwing yourself into them like there is no tomorrow. Go full tilt.

"Finally, do not waste time today worrying about yesterday or tomorrow. Yes, you *SHOULD* learn from your mistakes and successes. However, you must not become so bothered by them that you stop succeeding today. Additionally, you must never become so enamored with your past successes that you do not move on and succeed again today. Yes, you *SHOULD* plan for the future, but you must not spend so much time worrying about what might or might not happen tomorrow that you forget to act today. Most of the time, the things we worry about never happen. Most of the ones that do, do so because we worried them into existence. We can't do anything about yesterday or tomorrow. We can only act today. That is *PRIORITIZING.*"

"Alright, I get it," responded Sam. "I *SHALL* be the best me I *CAN.* I *SHALL* go beyond myself. However, in all of this, I must not get so bogged down in trying to do everything. I need to focus. I need to *PRIORITIZE* what I'm going to do and throw myself into those few things as hard as I *CAN* and not be distracted by the things that are not a part of those goals."

"I wish all of my students were as receptive and quick as you are, Sam," the *PROFESSOR* responded. "Here's your last homework assignment."

You SHALL Prioritize

What do you want to be said in your obituary?

What do you need to be doing now to make sure those things can be said when you die?

In what activities are you involved right now that do not add to what you believe is most important in your life? Write them down and mark through them-remove them.

What can you, by your strengths, do the most about?

"What do you think, Sam?" asked the *PRO-FESSOR*

"I don't know. This was like being with the *TRAINER*. It's overwhelming. It makes sense, but I'm not sure I *CAN* get my mind or my life around it all."

"That is a natural feeling to have, Sam. Turning your *SHOULDAS* into *SHALLS* is a lifetime process. You will not master it overnight. This is about progress not perfection. However, the more you work on it, the more meaningful your life will be. Go home tonight and watch <u>*Mr. Holland's Opus*</u> and do the rest of your homework. When you're done, break the molds and erase the prophecies that have grown up around your life, figure out where your strengths and your passions intersect, then figure out how to best use those to give to your family and your community. Do not let anyone or anything distract you from the *PRIORITIES* you land upon. Unless something so powerful and meaningful comes along that you are willing to realign your life and drop one of your other main focuses, let the new activity pass.

"Well, Sam. I think it is time for lunch. We have a great little restaurant in our student center. Plus, if you are with me, I *CAN* get you a discount. We'll get to know one another a little better and then I'll get you home where you *CAN* internalize all of this."

*****

While Sam and the *PROFESSOR* ate lunch, he pulled out the business card she gave him and looked at it again.

Your 3 "You Shalls"

You SHALL be the best You

You SHALL go beyond Yourself

You SHALL Prioritize

*****

Sam showed Susan his new card when he got home and explained it to her. She thought it was intriguing. In fact, she thought a lot of what Sam said applied to her as well. At least this time, she didn't try to discourage Sam from continuing to talk to Dave and his friends. She just hoped whatever Dave was going to do would happen soon. She was getting a little nervous.

Sam didn't wait for Dave to call him this time. In fact, the very next day he called Dave and asked to meet him for mid-morning coffee at *The Early Bird.*

While they drank their coffee, Dave asked, "Have you learned anything yet?"

"Yes, I have learned to turn my COULDAS into CANS, knowing that I can't do everything but I can do ANYTHINGG—with two Gs. Also, I have learned to turn my SHOULDAS into SHALLS by relieving some of the weight from my SHOULD-ers. My only concern is whether or not all of this will be just like all the other self-improvement fads I've been through. Like you said when I asked you last week, this is easy, but at the same time it's not. I can already tell I'm going to be my own worst enemy. How can I make sure to keep this up and GET TO DID?"

"Sam, that goes right into what you will learn from my third friend next week. We call him our *COACH*. The principles he teaches *WILL* keep you motivated and get you from *WOULDA* to *WILL*. In addition to that, don't forget we're still here as your support team. I still work with the *TRAINER*, the *PROFESSOR* and the *COACH* because I have down days as well. I don't know who said it, but I once heard a great quote. 'The only people who are always at their best are the mediocre ones.' We're striving to excel, but we will not always fly high. That's why we help each other. I hope in time, you *WILL* grow to be a help to me as well."

"I hope so too," Sam said with a smile. "I look forward to that day. I certainly appreciate all the help you're being right now. When do I get to meet the *COACH*?"

"I know you're anxious, Sam. However, let's stay on schedule. Soak in and think about what the *PROFESSOR* had to say. Do the homework she gave you. See how it goes along with what you learned from the *TRAINER* and next week you'll meet the *COACH* bright and early."

"I'll be there," Sam said brightly.

The COACH

From WOULDA to WILL

Sam had a great week. He began by sitting down with his 17 year old son, Scott.

"Son, I want to talk to you about college…"

"Look, Dad," Scott interjected, "I'm tired of arguing about this with you. I wish you'd just leave me alone about it. I don't want to go to your school and I'm not sure I even want to go to school period."

Sam took a deep, steadying breath, and said, "I know, and that's okay with me."

"What!?" Scott said with a double take at his dad. Then with a knowing smile, "Okay

Dad, what self-help, get what you want out of your kids, parenting book are you trying to use on me this week?"

"None," Sam said with a guess-I-deserved-that smile, "I've been talking with a couple of friends who've helped me see myself a little better. It's not fair or right of me to expect you to be me. You *SHOULD* be you. Don't get me wrong; nothing would make me happier than you going to my old school. And I still think it's a great choice. But the choice is yours, not mine. I just want you to know that whatever choices you make, so long as I don't think they are immoral, I *WILL* support you in them. Further, no matter what choices you make, even if I can't support them, I *WILL* always love you."

Scott just sat there looking shocked. Sam smiled and said, "If you want to talk to me more about what you plan to do after high school, just let me know. I love you, Scott." He hugged his son and then left Scott in stunned silence.

The most amazing thing about this was it lifted a great weight off Sam's shoulders. Realizing this choice was Scott's and not his meant he didn't have to worry about it anymore.

Further, even though Scott had not yet taken Sam up on his offer to talk more about his post-graduation plans, he was now talking to him with the warmth and respect he had before the college rift occurred.

While Sam was still in contact with his recruiter and keeping his eyes open for a good job opportunity, he was also developing plans to start his own business. Sam knew most people would think he was nuts starting his own landscaping business. After all, he thought, how many people actually like cutting grass and trimming shrubs? Yet, he did.

On top of that, he was actually excited about it. What made him most excited was that, for him, this wasn't really about making money, though he was honest and down to earth enough to know he did have to do that. His real thought was what his neighborhood would look like if he were able to take care of the landscaping. Further, he thought of all the people he could serve because they didn't like cutting the grass and digging flower beds.

There was no doubt about it, Sam was excited. He couldn't wait to meet with Dave's third friend—the *COACH*, whatever that was supposed to mean.

*****

111

The day finally arrived. Sam was waiting in Dave's driveway as the garage door lifted. He got in the car and said, "I'm ready for *The Early Bird.*"

Dave chuckled and headed down the now familiar road to his favorite coffee and breakfast spot. "How's your week been? You seem a little more up than two weeks ago."

"I'm on fire this week. I can't wait to meet your *COACH* friend and learn how to get from *WOULDA* to *WILL.*"

They pulled into *The Early Bird* parking lot and walked in, talking jovially. As they entered, Tammy and Melinda chimed, "Hey Dave. Hey Sam." Melinda added, "We have some great coffee cake today. You *SHOULD* branch out and try it."

"I *SHOULD* huh," Sam smiled and winked at Dave. "Well, if you say so, I guess I *SHALL.*"

As they waited for their coffee and breakfast, Sam recognized his oldest son's high school football coach sitting at the back table. "Is he your *COACH*?" he asked.

"That's him," Dave replied.

"You know, he's the winningest coach in our school's history."

"I know," Dave responded.

As they walked to the table, the COACH jumped up and grabbed Sam's hand, shaking it vigorously. "Hey Sam, I wondered if you were the Sam Dave had been talking about. I sure miss Sam, Jr. He helped make my first couple of years easy. I was always surprised he didn't stick with it in college. But, I guess each of us SHOULD do what we think is best."

"That's right," Dave interjected. "Not to change the subject, but what do you think about your upcoming season?"

They spent the next few minutes talking about football, their chances of winning State again, and generally just shooting the breeze.

Finally, Dave stood up and said, "Well guys, it's great looking into our local sports future, however, it's time for me to hit the road. I have my own future to work on today and so do you Sam."

He shook the COACH'S hand, turned to Melinda and said, "Can I have a piece of that coffee cake to go, please? Deborah will love it. Make it two, she doesn't have to know I ate one here." He received his order, waved goodbye to Sam and the COACH and headed out the door.

Sam turned to the *COACH*, "I had no idea you were the *COACH* Dave was talking about. I would have called you last week if I had. What's your connection with Dave?"

"That's a long story, Sam. Let's just say he helped me get through a tough time when I thought about giving up. He helped me get my *WOULDA* to *WILL* and has helped me keep it there ever since. If I didn't think the school board would cut my salary and give half of it to him, I'd let them know how much his influence has actually made our team what it is."

The *COACH* drained his coffee cup and then continued, "Let's get'r done. We've got a lot to talk about and I want to do it on familiar turf."

*****

The *COACH* took Sam to the high school. Instead of going to an office, he walked him onto the football field and said, "This is my sanctuary right here. This is always right. Struggle, survival, victory, and defeat. It's just a game, but I love it."

Sam laughed, "Isn't that from <u>Remember the Titans</u>?"

The *COACH* coughed slightly and said, "Yeah. Well...I've always wanted to say that. Anyway, let's get started. Head to the locker room. You remember where it is, don't you?"

As they walked, the *COACH* kept talking, "My job is to help you turn your *WOULDAS* into *WILLS*. Far too often there are all kinds of things we think we *WOULD* do, *BUT* something gets in the way. Looking back, we *WOULDA* studied harder in college, *BUT* we didn't know how important it was. We *WOULDA* saved more money for retirement, *BUT* it was too hard to make ends meet. We *WOULDA* gone further in our career, *BUT* it seemed like our boss was out to get us. *WOULDA, WOULDA, WOULDA*, before long our lives are just one big *BUT*.

"Up to this point you have learned what you *CAN* do; that was the *TRAINER'S* job. You have also learned what you really *SHOULD* do or as we say, *SHALL* do; that was the *PROFESSOR'S* job. Now we merge those two and focus on following through with what you *WILL* do. Are you ready?"

"I was ready last week. Let's get this show on the road," Sam answered as they walked into the locker room.

"The keys I'm going to teach you are the same ones I pass on to my football team. Take a look at the sign above the door. My guys see it every time they head out to the field."

Sam turned around and looked up to see a sign that read:

Make the *PLAY*

"That's great for football," Sam retorted, "but what does that have to do with me? Wait...let me guess—you have a card that explains it."

The *COACH* laughed and pulled a card out of a small rack on the wall beside the door. It read:

Make the

*P*assion

*L*ook to the future

*A*ccept no excuses

*Y*es men

"What is it with you people and acrostics?" Sam quipped.

"They make life fun. Who knows? Maybe one day Dave will write a book about *GETTING TO DID* and all the hard work will already be done. Anyway, this is the key to turning your *WOULDAS* into *WILLS*. This is the key to maintaining motivation."

"Alright, what does it mean? I'm not sure I like the sound of 'Yes Men,'" Sam replied.

"We'll get to them in a minute.

"First, we have to start with *PASSION*."

"I think I have that one down," Sam interrupted. "This goes along with what the *PROFESSOR* taught me. She said she was stepping on your field a little bit. *PASSION* means doing what I am *PASSIONATE* about, what I enjoy and can really get into. It makes sense to teach this while we talk about motivation as well. After all, it's a lot easier to be motivated doing something you love than something you hate."

"Allow me to illustrate," the *COACH* added. "When I started off in college, I was majoring in Business and Marketing. My plan was to make big money in some Fortune 500 company. I had it all mapped out. You may love that sort of thing Sam, however, about half way through my junior year, I realized I hated what I was doing. That explained why I was always on the verge of getting failed for missing too many classes and why I started getting low C's when I was usually a pretty solid A and B student. I was talking to an older friend of mine who worked as a high paid accountant for a local company. I asked him how he liked his job. He said, 'I hate it. But it keeps the family fed.' He looked miserable. In that moment, I decided I didn't want to live like him.

"Getting to where I am now was a bit of a journey but this is where I *SHOULD* be. Most days, I can't wait to get to work. It's more like playing than work to me. I love what I do. I love the practices, the games and I love working with the kids. I feel like I'm making a difference in their lives. Sure, there are some down days. But most of the time, being motivated comes naturally because I absolutely love what I do. I have PASSION.

"One of the areas where PASSION is most helpful is in accomplishing those self-discipline habits that are so easy to overlook for a few days and then stop completely. I love to exercise and I love to be healthy. I start most days with running, swimming or something to get my heart pumping. That's easy for me 'cause I'm PASSIONATE about exercise and health.

"My sister, on the other hand, hates exercise. I helped her get started running. She got so upset, wondering when it would be fun, natural or easy like the running magazines said it would. As I was helping her get into the habit I tried everything. I tried systems of rewards and punishments. I tried getting her to read about healthy people and unhealthy people and what their lives are like when they're older. I tried guilt. I tried praise.

"Then one night she had me and my family over for dinner. I was in a slightly grumpy mood over issues at the school. Therefore, regrettably I was being a little short about everything. As usual, the issue of the kids growing quickly came up and she said something about her seven year old's graduation being just around the corner. Without any real intention of trying to impact her health and mostly because I was irritated anyway I somewhat caustically said, 'I hope you're still around for it.'

> "Work to tie those pesky habits of self-discipline about which you can hardly be *PASSIONATE* to something about which you are *PASSIONATE*. Then be amazed at how much easier those issues become."

"The conversation that ensued was life-changing for her. For all we had tried, she never made the connection between her health and her relationship with her children. If she is not *PASSIONATE* about her health or exercise, she is extremely *PASSIONATE* about her family. When she made that connection, the *PASSION* for health and exercise was suddenly in place. She can't run circles around me, but she's sure trying.

"Work to tie those pesky habits of self-discipline about which you can hardly be *PASSIONATE* to something about which you are *PASSIONATE*. Then be amazed at how much easier those issues become."

"That's powerful," Sam replied. "I've never thought about that before. The health and kid thing, that is. Maybe all of this is going to help me with more than just my financial life."

"Let me explain the other benefit of *PASSION*. Not only does it help you get up in the morning, it also helps you strive for excellence. There are coaches who are just making a paycheck. They played football in high school and thought it would be an easy job. You can tell their teams; they have the losing records. The ones with *PASSION* push that extra mile. Since they are so *PASSIONATE* about what they do, they want to be the best they can possibly be. Good enough is never good enough for the *PASSIONATE*. They don't settle for minimum job requirements. They go above and beyond for the sake of their *PASSION*.

"If you're going to Make the *PLAY*, Sam, you've got to have *PASSION*."

"*PASSION*. Got it," Sam responded.

"Listen, I have some exercises for you to work through this week," the *COACH* said handing Sam a piece of paper.

PASSION

Pretend you have it to do all over again and money is no issue, what *WILL* you do?

What do you most regret not doing so far?

What work provides you the greatest satisfaction?

Taking it a step further, what part of the work provides you with the greatest satisfaction?

Why aren't you doing more of the things you mentioned above? Get with it!

Looking up from the paper, Sam asked, "Okay, have *PASSION*. What about *LOOK TO THE FUTURE*? I already talked about planning and goal-setting with the *TRAINER*. Is that what this is about?"

"Not quite. Planning, or as the *TRAINER* put it, *NEXT STEP THINKING*, gets you from *COULDA* to *CAN*. We're talking about motivation here, going from *WOULDA* to *WILL*. *LOOK TO THE FUTURE* is really about refusing to be governed by the present moment.

"Wait a minute," Sam said shaking his head. "The *TRAINER* and the *PROFESSOR* both said all I had was today and that I needed to live in the present moment. How can you say I'm not supposed to be governed by it?"

"We live in the moment, Sam, but we aren't governed by it. That is, there are some things we do in the present moment that we don't like because we know where they lead. No matter how *PASSIONATE* you are, there are always aspects of your work and life you won't be *PASSIONATE* about. I hate parent/teacher conferences. I hate grading tests and papers in the Math class I have to teach if I want to coach. What helps me keep going and plugging away through these drudgeries? *LOOKING TO THE FUTURE*. I constantly remind myself of the rewards of doing the parts that I don't like about this job. First, if I want to keep looking forward to the parts I do like, I have to do the others as well. Second, even though I don't like them, I realize they're part of the process that accomplishes what I am *PAS-SIONATE* about. Those conferences help keep the parents involved in their kids' lives. They help the parents know where I can see their kids going in the future. And they help the parents and me get on the same team. While I prefer coaching football to teaching Math, I can see that most of my guys aren't going to make a living playing football and even the one or two that ever will are going to need life skills to be successful.

"My job is not well done just because my guys have a fun, winning season. My job is well done when they're well prepared to go out and *PASSIONATELY* pursue their life's course. On those days when I don't feel like teaching Math or hav-ing the parent/teacher conference, I look down the road at the kids' lives. *LOOKING TO THE FUTURE* motivates me to Make the *PLAYS* I don't like making.

> "We have to learn not to be governed by that moment. We have to *LOOK TO THE FUTURE* and remember where all of this is heading."

"Further, let's face it, even with the stuff

we are *PASSIONATE* about, we all have down days. My team doesn't win State every year. We don't win every game. And we don't always have great practices. Some days, weeks and years, things just don't go right. The players may not be the high caliber we need. We may have made a staffing error. I may be sick. Who knows, maybe it's just raining too much. Nobody soars on an emotional high all the time; not even in their areas of *PASSION*. We have to learn not to be governed by that moment. We have to *LOOK TO THE FUTURE* and remember where all of this is heading. This is big picture thinking. Don't get bogged down by the bad moments, days, weeks or even years. My father-in-law had a lot of bad moments. I always remember how he faced them. He always said, 'This too shall pass.' Don't get bogged down it. Just recognize if you're working to make the *PLAY* these down times won't last.

"*LOOK TO THE FUTURE* and remember what the whole journey is about. That will help you Make the *PLAY* even when you don't feel like it.

"Are you with me so far, Sam?"

"Sure, this all makes sense. I have to learn to be motivated to Make the *PLAY*. That is a lot easier if I love what I'm doing, if I'm *PASSIONATE* about it. However, no matter how much *PASSION* I have, there will be down times. To keep motivated during those times I have to *LOOK TO THE FUTURE*."

"Good," the *COACH* said, "Now I know why Sam, Jr. was always so quick to catch on. Here's another exercise for you to work through this week."

LOOK TO THE FUTURE

Be honest, what parts of the work you do are you not so *PASSIONATE* about?

How do these not-so-desirable parts allow you to do the work you are *PASSIONATE* about?

How do these not-so-desirable aspects help accomplish the goal about which you are *PASSIONATE*?

What will be the end result and the rewards that eventually come from keeping on even during the tough times and throughout the unlikable parts of what you are doing?

"Alright we have talked about PASSION and *LOOKING TO THE FUTURE*. Now you must learn to *ACCEPT NO EXCUSES*," the COACH began again. "Even the best laid plans get old from time to time and you just don't want to follow through. This is an agreement issue. You have agreed to and committed yourself to a course of action. You must *ACCEPT NO EXCUSES* until you have followed through. We have to realize just about everything we do is a choice. You did not have to come here today; you chose to. You did not have to work your job for all those years; you chose to. You do not have to do anything about your situation right now; you are choosing to. *EXCUSES* are nothing more than blaming something or someone for our carelessness or wrong choices.

"Think of a few excuses you've made when you didn't pull through like you were supposed to. Have you ever excused yourself for not coming through on a project by saying, 'I'm sorry, I just didn't have enough time'? What would you have said if the person questioning you had asked, 'What did you spend your time doing instead of working on this project? Did you keep up with your favorite television show?' Or have you ever fallen short and responded, 'I'm sorry, I just forgot'? Why didn't you act on it immediately or write it down? Do not tolerate *EXCUSES* from yourself. Listen, I'm not saying be a tyrant to everyone else. I'm telling you to hold yourself to higher standards and *ACCEPT NO EXCUSES*."

Sam jumped in, "But aren't there times when you really have a good *EXCUSE*?"

"No, there are never good *EXCUSES*. There are, at times, good *REASONS*. There is a difference. In a game, if one of my receivers gets the ball in his hands and drops it, he will be running laps. I *ACCEPT NO EXCUSES* for that. I don't want to hear how wet the ball was or how he was distracted or how he forgot what pattern he was running. Those are all *EXCUSES*. I want to hear he caught the ball. On the other hand, if the quarterback throws it wild or if the defense just makes a good play, I don't hold that over my receivers' heads. Those are *REASONS*. Sometimes my team just gets outplayed on the field. If the other team's defense was just making all the right moves and their offense was working tight, I can handle getting beat. That is a *REASON* for losing. On the other hand, if my guys were sloppy and not putting forth their best effort out there on the field, everything they will say in the locker room afterwards is just an *EXCUSE*. I don't tolerate that sort of behavior from my football team or myself.

"There is another aspect of ACCEPT NO EXCUSES. No matter how much you plan, prepare and protect yourself, there are going to be some failures. I'm sure one of the others already told you this, however, the only people who never fail are the ones who don't try anything. ACCEPT NO EXCUSES means when you fail you don't duck out on your responsibilities. You don't make up lame excuses to explain away your failure. Take a good long hard look at what you did and what obstacles you faced. Then find the REASONS you failed and try again, working to overcome those REASONS. Use your failures as a springboard for future successes.

> "Use your failures as a springboard for future successes."

"At the same time, don't think that ACCEPT NO EXCUSES means you have to beat yourself up every time you make a mistake. I remember one time when I learned I was doing this to myself. I missed a turn and the first thing out of my mouth was, 'You idiot!' But it struck me. I wasn't an idiot. I'm actually a pretty smart guy. I just had my mind on other things and missed my turn. I did what all humans do. I made a mistake. Here was the great thing. I learned that day to make a u-turn and learn from my mistake to do better the next time. I *ACCEPTED NO EXCUSES*. I didn't try to blame anyone else or anything else. I owned my own mistake and learned from it to do better the next time.

"If you're going to *COACH* for very long, you have to do this. When I lose a game, I don't get to say, 'That's it, I'm never playing that team again.' In fact, I may have to play them again this year. That means I get out the video and go over the game, play by play, looking for mistakes and weaknesses. At the same time, I look for what worked. In other words, I find the *REASONS* we lost in order to fix what is broken before we play that team again. I *ACCEPT NO EXCUSES*. I certainly discipline my team for sloppy play, but I don't beat them up or call them names for making mistakes. I encourage us all to own our responsibilities, to learn from the mistakes and move on.

"I imagine you encountered the need for this philosophy time and again in the sales world."

"You know it. If there was ever anything that clued me in to know someone wasn't going to cut it as a salesman, it was how they handled rejection," Sam explained. "Some viewed it as a springboard, a place to learn. Some took it personally, thinking it meant they were failures. I'll tell you what though, my best salesmen did not just use their failures as learning experiences. They would even review their successes with their co-workers and supervisors, looking at what worked and what may have almost been a hindrance."

"You're two steps ahead of me, Sam. If you're going to grow, don't just look at your failures, examine your successes. Is there anything you can do to make it work more smoothly? Was there something different about this team or that customer that made this approach work when it didn't or wouldn't work another time? Either way, you're always working to rule out *EXCUSES*. You can't Make the *PLAY* if you are always making *EXCUSES* for why you're not making it, won't make it or didn't make it.

"This really cuts to the heart of the *COULDAS, SHOULDAS* and *WOULDAS* and your big *BUTS*. When we find ourselves saying those, we are usually making *EXCUSES*."

"Now you're making me feel small. I don't know how many *EXCUSES* I've accepted throughout my life. When you put it like this, it makes perfect sense. I'm going to work on that," Sam said thoughtfully. "Where's my homework on this one?"

ACCEPT NO EXCUSES

Be *HONEST*, what *EXCUSES* have you accepted in the past?

What obstacles do you see to your upcoming plans? What obstacles have stopped you before?

Now that you have identified upcoming obstacles, how *WILL* you overcome them?

Examine some of your successes. What made them successful? What might have been a hindrance even in those successes?

After reading the questions on the paper, he asked, "Okay, I get the *PASSION*, *LOOKING TO THE FUTURE*, and *ACCEPTING NO EXCUSES*. But what is up with this *YES MEN* thing? I've always hated that."

The *COACH* responded, "Yeah, Dave told me you were already upset about that one. The normal connotation of *YES MEN* is dreadful. We don't want people who just always say, 'Yes,' even when they disagree in order to get on our good side. That, however, is not what I mean by *YES MEN*. We want people who will challenge our thinking and expand our vision.

"These *YES MEN* are people with whom you surround yourself to encourage you and hold you accountable. They are the people who tell you, '*YES*, you *CAN*,' when you are thinking, 'No, I can't.' They tell you, '*YES*, you *SHALL*,' when you are thinking, 'No, I shall not.' They tell you, '*YES*, you *WILL*,' when you are thinking, 'No, I won't.'

"Your *YES MEN* are your accountability partners. Dave and I get together regularly along with the *TRAINER* and the *PROFESSOR* to act as each other's *YES MEN*. Further, we get together with many of the other people we have helped along the way.

"I hope you don't think it'll be a cake walk from this point on. I can't tell you how many people I've had this conversation with who end up settling for mediocrity in their lives. They don't step up to the plate. When you talk to them today, they've just grown their big ol' *BUTS* back again. Without fail, each one started back into their old habits of *COULDA, SHOULDA* and *WOULDA* by neglecting their relationship with their *YES MEN*.

"As you pick out your *YES MEN*, don't pick out the ones we often think of as *YES MEN*, the ones afraid to state their convictions and disagree when it's necessary. They won't help you. Pick the ones who'll push you. Pick the ones who'll force you to get up when you have fallen. Pick the ones who'll question you and make you clarify your vision and your course of action. Pick the ones who'll *ACCEPT NO EXCUSES*. But make sure to pick out *YES MEN* who are willing to say '*YES*, you *CAN*,' even when no one else has before.

"When you have established your council of *YES MEN*, be completely open and honest with them. Let them know your plans, dreams and visions. Let them know the obstacles you see and the struggles you face. Let them know your fears. Then listen respectfully to their advice. Remember, it's just that, advice. You *SHOULD* still be you and you must make your final choices. Good *YES MEN* will *AC-CEPT NO EXCUSES* from you, not even, 'I did what you *YES MEN* said I *SHOULD.*'

"Here are the benefits of *YES MEN*. First, two heads are better than one. Even with all of your *INSIGHT* into your work and life, it's still hard to read the label when you're inside the bottle. It's always good to get advice and counsel from others with differing perspectives.

"Second, you'll be surprised how often your network of *YES MEN* can actually help you with your projects in practical ways by connecting you with others or with needed resources. For instance, when I first started working with this high school, you may remember the team had maintained a losing record for several years. The school board had cut the budget. We were in desperate need of new equipment and didn't have the funds."

"Oh yeah, I remember that," Sam said. "I remember little Sam complaining about some of the outdated and dilapidated equipment. One of the local sporting goods stores stepped in and made some donations didn't it?"

"That's right. What you don't know is those donations came because I laid out my troubles to my *YES MEN* council. The *TRAINER* had a connection with the upper crust at that store. Dave had an accountant friend who explained the tax advantages of making such a donation. Voilà, our equipment issues were resolved.

"The third benefit from *YES MEN* is they help pick you up when you fall down. Before I moved here, I had an experience so devastating I was ready to throw in the towel. I had made a few mistakes in my first head coaching job. Instead of letting me learn from them and grow, one of my assistant coaches, a man I thought was a friend, went behind my back to get me ousted so he could have the job. It was my introduction to another aspect I hate about this job—school politics. I was down and the ref had counted to 9. That was when Dave really came into my life. He had been my landlord for a few years. One day he was just checking out his property and struck up a conversation with me. I guess I needed someone to talk to because I just opened up to him like he was my best friend. He taught me about *GETTING TO DID* and ever since he has acted as my *YES MAN*, picked me up and helped me move on. I'm just going to tell you, you can't replace that or manufacture it on your own.

"Fourth, maybe I think this because I'm such a people person, but life is just more fun when you're sharing it with others. Your council of *YES MEN* gives you people to laugh and cry with. It gives you people to support and people who support you. It gives you people who will pat you on your back when you do well and kick you in the backside when you slack off. It just makes life more interesting and more fun.

"Finally, when it's time to do battle and go toe to toe with the ones who'll try to knock you down and keep you from reaching your goals, your *YES MEN* provide you with support and strength you *WILL* never have alone.

"My game is a game of *YES MEN*. I have yet to see the one man football team. No *PLAY* in my game is ever made by a single player. I never let my team forget that. We have to support each other, defend each other and bust heads for each other. In the end, I'm convinced there've been some games we won simply because we '*YES* we *CAN*ned' each other through it.

"Here's your final exercise. It's pretty simple."

YES MEN

Make a list below of the people who can help you *GET TO DID.*
Who can help you turn your *COULDAS* into *CANS*?
Who can help you turn your *SHOULDAS* into *SHALLS*?
Who can help you turn your WOULDAS *into* WILLS?

How will you let these people hold you accountable?

As Sam looked up from the paper, the COACH asked, "What do you think, Sam?"

"This is great," replied Sam excitedly, "I'm on fire. I *CAN* Make the *PLAY* right now on sheer *PASSION* alone. You, however, have helped me realize it won't always be like this. I have to be prepared for those moments when I don't feel like Making the *PLAY*. I need to *LOOK TO THE FUTURE*, thinking in the big picture to stay motivated even when I'm not on fire about what I am doing at the moment. I must *ACCEPT NO EXCUSES* but face up to my responsibilities and push on to success. Finally, I need to get a council of *YES MEN* who'll push me where and when I need to be pushed."

"You've got it. Any questions?"

"Yeah, *WILL* you be one of my *YES MEN*?"

The COACH grabbed Sam's hand and shook it, saying, "I thought you'd never ask. How about we go grab a bite of lunch and have our first *YES MEN* council meeting?"

"Sounds great," Sam said. As he walked to the *COACH'S* car, he looked again at the card the *COACH* had given him.

Make the

*P*assion

*L*ook to the future

*A*ccept no excuses

*Y*es men

*****

Sam was so excited as he shared what he learned with Susan she could not make even one objection to what he had to say. To Sam's pleasant surprise, when he finished his ecstatic description, she said, "I *WILL* be happy to let you follow whatever course you think you *SHOULD* on two conditions."

"Really? What are they?" Sam asked.

"First, let me be one of your *YES MEN* and keep me informed about what's going on. Second, let me live by the same principles."

"That's awesome, as long as you promise to really be a *YES MAN* or perhaps I should say, *YES WOMAN*. I don't mind if you keep me in reality, but will you be willing to dream with me and make those dreams realities?"

"I'll put it this way," Susan responded thoughtfully, "I don't think I am as far down this *GETTING TO DID* path as you. But I promise to keep walking it with you."

Sam jumped up and kissed his wife. It had been a while since they shared a kiss quite like that one.

The Council

Getting to Did

It was an exciting day for Sam. He was having his first real *YES MEN* council meeting. He was going to meet with Dave, his *TRAINER*, his *PROFESSOR*, his *COACH* and, as agreed, his *WIFE.* They were meeting, of course, at *The Early Bird*.

After introducing Susan to the rest of the council and vice versa, Sam said, "Well guys, I don't know exactly how one of these meetings *SHOULD* be run. However, I'm sure none of you wants to sit here all day. Let's get this meeting moving forward."

Dave said, "Before we get to your items of business. I just want to find out what you have learned from my three friends."

"Wow," Sam responded, "I've learned so much from you all. Answering that question could keep us here for hours. I *WILL* sum it up. The fact is, you have taught me to get rid of my big *BUT* and live without regrets.

"The *TRAINER* has taught me how to turn my *COULDAS* into *CANS*. I have learned that I can't do E*VERYTHING*, but I can do A*NY-THINGG*."

Sam pulled out the card he had laminated so it would stand up to his constant referral.

You can't do EVERYTHING,
But you *CAN* do ***ANYTHINGG***!

ATTITUDE

NEXT STEP THINKING

YOUR STRENGTHS

TIME

HONESTY

INSIGHT

NEVER QUIT

GROWTH

GOALS

Sam continued, "The *PROFESSOR* has helped me remove the heavy burden from my *SHOULD*-ers and turned my *SHOULDAS* into *SHALLS*. Three *SHALLS* in fact."

Sam pulled out another laminated card and placed it on the table.

Your 3 "You Shalls"

You SHALL be the best You

You SHALL go beyond Yourself

You SHALL Prioritize

As the council members smiled, Sam went on. "The *COACH* taught me how to stay motivated and turn my *WOULDAS* into *WILLS*. In great football *COACH* fashion, he taught me how to always Make the *PLAY*."

With a flourish, Sam produced one more laminated card and laid it beside the other two.

Make the

*P*assion

L ook to the future

*A*ccept no excuses

*Y*es men

"In short," Sam concluded, "you all have taught me how to *GET TO DID*. And I am so excited to tell you about what I have already done...*DID*."

At this point, Dave jumped in. "Before you tell us that, I have one more lesson for you. It is the final lesson that gets you from *COULDA*, *SHOULDA* and *WOULDA* to *CAN*, *SHALL* and *WILL*. It removes all that excess flab from your big *BUT*. It *GETS TO DID*."

"What else can there be?" Sam questioned.

"*JUST DID IT*," Dave replied.

"Don't you mean 'Just Do It'?," Sam asked perplexed, a feeling he had gotten used to throughout this entire learning process.

"No. That's the Nike slogan. This is our final lesson. *JUST DID IT*. All the planning, counseling and motivating only *GETS TO DID* when you actually *DID IT*. After we leave this meeting, you have to go out and do it or, as we like to say, *DID IT*. We say it that way because speaking in the past tense demonstrates our commitment to making our goals realities and points out that until we actually *DID IT*, we haven't accomplished anything.

"I am excited for you, Sam, and you, Susan. No matter what choices you make from this point on, whether they're the choices I would make or not, if you're following these principles, you're going to have a new life. We are here to help you *GET TO DID*. Now, what did you want to share with us about your plans?"

For the next hour, Sam shared his plans with his council. He had decided to press on with his plans to start his own landscaping business. He explained how he was going to be able to start out without incurring any debt and then progress over the next five years to bigger and bigger business. He had even worked out a plan for hiring workers and then managers as his business grew. He talked about how he was going to grow his clientele through direct mail marketing, which he had used successfully as a salesman. Sam's *PASSION* oozed for an hour.

The council listened intently. Dave, the *TRAINER*, the *PROFESSOR* and the *COACH* were excited for Sam and thought about how meaningful it was that they had been a part of helping a man who had felt defeated and desperate become the man who sat before them speaking with excitement and confidence. Susan, also listening intently, was excited to see such new life in her husband and was also excitedly thinking about the journey she could see stretching out before her as she learned to *GET TO DID* along with Sam.

When Sam was finished, the *YES MEN* plied him with questions to clarify his vision, gave him advice and then offered some practical help.

Dave, having seen how Sam manicured his own lawn, was willing to hire Sam as his landscaper on the spot. He even expressed that when Sam's business had grown enough to cover the work and the contract was up with his, Dave's, present lawn maintenance crew at his apartments and restaurants, he would let Sam bid on those jobs as well.

The *PROFESSOR* said she would put a word in for Sam when the university worked on the next year's budget for landscaping. She told him to start working up his proposal.

The *COACH* said, "Hey, I'm living on a teacher's salary. I have to cut my own grass. However, I know some people that might be interested. I *WILL* let them know."

All in all, Sam's first council meeting was a raging success. Sam and Susan left the meeting ready to get to work and ready to *GET TO DID*.

Sam's Rebuilt World

Sam continued with his plans. He turned his *COULDAS* into *CANS*, his *SHOULDAS* into *SHALLS* and his *WOULDAS* into *WILLS*. He got rid of his big *BUT*. He was consistently able to *GET TO DID*.

Don't misunderstand. His life was no bowl of cherries. He had struggles. He had ups and downs. Some days, weeks and years were worse than others. He had times when he considered throwing in the towel. His *YES MEN* council helped him through those days.

In time, his business expanded. He employed others and eventually trained managers to start extensions of his company in neighboring cities. He began to write do-it-yourself manuals that he sold online providing residual income beyond his own personal landscaping work.

Sam began to teach these principles to his family, friends and employees. He was convinced that the more people he could help *GET TO DID*, the better his community would be. Sam found himself a part of several *YES MEN* councils. One of his greatest pleasures was seeing someone else *GET TO DID*.

He continued to celebrate his successes with his council. He even became a trusted advisor for each of these people who had been a help to him.

To each person he taught, he explained that the specifics in their life would differ. They *SHOULD* follow their own life's course. But the principles would be the same, whether they started a business, found a job or just needed help with a particular project.

Sam's biggest desire today is propagating the *GETTING TO DID* message as far and wide as possible. He is asking you to help. Don't hoard this message. *GO BEYOND YOURSELF* and share it with others.

This is the end of
Sam's story.

Hopefully,
it is the beginning of
yours.

LaVergne, TN USA
11 February 2010
172797LV00004B/24/P